WITHDRAWN

Jaguar of Sweet Laughter

NEW & SELECTED POEMS

Jaguar
of
Sweet
Laughter

NEW & SELECTED POEMS

Diane Ackerman

Random House
New York

Some of the poems in this work were originally published in the
following journals: *American Poetry Review, Amicus, The Atlantic
Monthly, Chelsea, Denver Quarterly, First Love, The Gettysburg Review,
Kenyon Review, Michigan Quarterly Review, The New York Times Book
Review, Parnassus: Poetry in Review, The Planetry Report, Poetry, Prairie
Schooner, Travel-Holiday,* and *Star Date.*

Library of Congress Cataloguing-in-Publication Data

Ackerman, Diane.
Jaguar of sweet laughter :
new and selected poems /
by Diane Ackerman.
p. cm.
ISBN 0-394-57645-4
I. Title.
PS3551.C48J34 1990
811'.54—dc20   90-48243

Manufactured in the United States of America
24689753
First Edition

For Paul,
master fictioneer,
with love

A creation myth found in the Popol Vuh, a book sacred to the Maya, tells of Jaguar of Sweet Laughter, the first human creature to appear on earth, a strange being who could speak.

Acknowledgments

I'm grateful to the editors of the following journals for first publishing these poems:

The American Poetry Review: "Sister Juana Inés de la Cruz, Hearing that Her Lover, Giorgio, Has Drowned"

The Atlantic Monthly: "Halley's Comet"

Chelsea: "White Flag," "Air Show in Barbados"

Denver Quarterly: "The Archbishop of Puebla Weighs Sister Juana Inés de la Cruz's Passion for Study," "An Italian Courtier Pines for His Mistress, the Learned Nun, Sister Juana Inés de la Cruz"

The Gettysburg Review: "Wanderlust," "Transition"

Kenyon Review: "Intensive Care," "Soft Lens," "At Walt Whitman's Birthplace"

Michigan Quarterly Review: "Grand Canyon," "Nightletter to Loren Eiseley"

The New York Times Book Review: "Still Life"

Paris Reveiw: "A Pilot's Pay," "Antartica Offers Scott Her Latern"

Parnassus: Poetry in Review: "On Looking into Sylvia Plath's Copy of Goethe's *Faust*"

The Planetary Report: "Wanderlust," "We Are Listening," "Halley's Comet"

Poetry: "Beija-Flor," "St. Louis Botanical Gardens," "Letter of Retainer," "We Are Listening," "Lament of the Banyan Tree"

Poly: "The white hypnosis"

Prairie Schooner: "Opening the Locket," "Pumping Iron," "Poem in Winter," "The Manure Gatherers," "In the Green Purse of the Yard This Loose Red Change," "Lady Canute," "Portrait without Pose," "Dinner at the Waldorf," "Song of the Trilobite"

Star Date: "We Are Listening"

Travel-Holiday: "Coboclo," "Where the Sun Dines"

Contents

New
Poems

INTENSIVE CARE

In the antiseptic Eden,
your small light burns:
a green dot
that carried you
across two continents,
from coal-mining village,
cricket for the county,
and Oxford ribbons,
to picturesque America,
where life is a bonfire
and a man's heart
does not attack him.

For fourteen years
I've huddled close
to that heart
strangers decode
by echo-scan
and oscilloscope.
The smocked magicians
of rhythm
turn level eyes
to your pounding
electricity.

Midnight.
All our totemic animals
are asleep:
the kangaroos,
the panther,
the harvest mouse,
the camel,
the prairie dogs,
the lion:

the full bestiary
of our animal love.
The doctors, your mother,
and your poet all sleep.
Only your heart
lies awake.

With ink and a stylus
it scratches out
a story,
speaking its dialect
all quiver and pump.
You may sleep,
but the novelist
in your chest
never sleeps,
minting yarns
bold, stylish, and macabre.

When it gabbles,
alarms ring
up and down the ward.
"Are you all right?"
a nurse wakes you to ask,
and you know your heart
has been rambling again
while you slept,
slipping off the hoods
and turning all
its falcons loose.

At home alone
across the lake,
a darkness too possible
invades the house
and my chest becomes

a suit of armor
shrunk tight by worry.
Mi casa es su casa.

I want to fly
to that ward
black as a mine shaft
where you drowse,
thatched deep
in wire and electrode,
still gamely
performing
a ventriloquism
from the heart:
on a monitor
your small light
glowing like radium.

WE ARE LISTENING

I

As our metal eyes wake
to absolute night,
where whispers fly
from the beginning of time,
we cup our ears to the heavens.
We are listening

on the volcanic rim of Flagstaff
and in the fields beyond Boston,
in a great array that blooms
like coral from the desert floor,
on highwire webs patrolled
by computer spiders in Puerto Rico.

We are listening for a sound
beyond us, beyond sound,

searching for a lighthouse
in the breakwaters of our uncertainty,
an electronic murmur,
a bright, fragile *I am.*

Small as tree frogs
staking out one end
of an endless swamp,
we are listening
through the longest night
we imagine, which dawns
between the life and times of stars.

II

Our voice trembles
with its own electric,
we who mood like iguanas,
we who breathe sleep
for a third of our lives,
we who heat food
to the steaminess of fresh prey,
then feast with such
good manners it grows cold.

In mind gardens
and on real verandas
we are listening,
rapt among the Persian lilacs
and the crickets,
while radio telescopes
roll their heads, as if in anguish.

With our scurrying minds
and our lidless will
and our lank, floppy bodies
and our galloping yens
and our deep, cosmic loneliness
and our starboard hearts
where love careens,
we are listening,
the small bipeds
with the giant dreams.

THE DARK NIGHT OF
THE HUMMINGBIRD

A lot of hummingbirds die in their sleep,
dreaming of nectar-sweet funnels they sipped.
Moth-light, they swiveled at succulent
blooms, all flash and ripple—like sunset,
but delicate, probing, excitable,
their wings a soft fury of iridescence,
their hearts beating like a tiny drumroll
fourteen hundred times a minute,
their W-shaped tongues, drawing nectar
down each groove, whispering: *wheels within wheels.*
By day, hovering hard, they fly nowhere
at speed, swilling energy. But to refuel,
they must eat, and to eat they must hover,
burning more air than a sprinting impala.

So, in the dark night of the hummingbird,
while lilies lather sweetly in the rain,
the hummingbird rests near collapse,
its quick pulse halved, its rugged breath shallow,
its W-shaped tongue, & bright as Cassiopeia,
now mumbling words like *wistful* and *wan.*
The world at once drug, anthem, bright lagoon,
where its heart knew all the Morse codes
for rapture, pales into a senseless twilight.
It can't store enough fuel to last the night
and hoist it from its well of dreams
to first light trembling on wet fuchsia,
nor break the hard promise life always keeps.
A lot of hummingbirds die in their sleep.

WHITE FLAG

A benediction before nightfall,
    she enters the yard
  for some deerfelt purpose,
though she knows humans
     mark this territory as theirs
    with footfall, laughter,
and otherworldly spoors
    of shovel, rake,
    chair, or leather ball.

Yesterday, she ambled over
    the swell in the lawn
  and found us at swim
(just two floating heads:
    big-eyed, whisper-hissing),
  and puzzled for some time,
her ears hunting
    like radar dishes,
  then slouched down the yard,
paused, coiled tight,
    and leapt away like a shout.

She often gets the jitters
    and stares deep into my window
  where nightmare lurks
behind hallucinating glass.
    Mind you, I'm no stranger,
  dim as a wolf pack. She eyes me
through light foliage
    when I'm grazing wild strawberries,
  or bathing in blue
off-smelling water,
    or raking high apples down
    for her in bud-summer,

or shoveling apples from crusty snow
      in late autumn.

But she always waits for me
      to drift indoors
    before risking the yard's open alert
and the red siren of the trees:
      twin galaxies of fruit
    ripening toward her long feast,
September. She brings me
      the dotted surprise
    of her fawns, and once a lame buck
shot out of season.

Over the months, her soft belly
      has bent the fence low
    between us. But tonight she stole in
under the hem of a large fir,
      sudden, impossible,
    live gossip from a far country,
and scouted the pool first
      —no hidden humans—
    then began that anxious browse
she does, at peace but wary,
      grazing at half-alert.

Burnt-red as an Aztec god,
      she found me reflecting
    in a near window, tail-flagged
a semaphore quick as a sting,
      and followed with a head-to-toe
    twitch arpeggio, trotted
down the yard where boundaries
      are softer, then leapt back
    into a pandemonium of green.

ON LOOKING INTO SYLVIA PLATH'S COPY OF GOETHE'S *FAUST*

You underlined the "jugglery of flame"
with ink sinewy and black as an ocelot.
Pensive about ash, you ran to detail,
you ran the mad sweetshop of the soul,
keen for Faust's appetite, not Helen's beauty.
No stranger to scalpel or garden,
you collected bees, knew how to cook,
dressed simply, and undressed the flesh
in word mirrors. Armed and dangerous
with the nightstick of desire,
you became the doll of insight we knew
to whom nearly all lady poets write,
a morbid Santa Claus who could die on cue.
You had the gift of rage, and a savage wistfulness.
You wanted life to derange you,
to sample its real muscle, you wanted
to be a word on the lips of the abyss.
You wanted to unlock the weather system
in your cells, and one day you did.

I never loved the pain you wore as a shroud,
but your keen naturalist's eye,
avid and roaming, your nomad curiosity,
and the cautionless ease with which your mind
slid into the soft flesh of an idea.
I thought you found serenity in the plunge
of a hot image into cool words.
I thought you took the pledge
that sunlight makes to living things,
could be startled to joy
by the green epaulets of a lily.
But you were your own demonology,
balancing terror's knife on one finger,
until you numbed, and the edge fell free.

HALLEY'S COMET

I

A nomad roaming
the starlit halls
of evening,

in a cold sweat
from some early tantrum
of light,

it bolts toward
the glow of a dashing
blue planet,

ancient, glacial,
always in a lather,

to blaze its loop
through the pastures
of the Sun.

A rumor at first
on a thousand
glass lips,

it passes
like winter
from land to land,

stretching a long arm
around the shivers
of the night,

waving its white
plume—
cascading lilies—

signing the blue
petition of each day
with its haste.

II

Dropped out of nothing,
it will return
to nothing,

but, in between,
toast the miracle waters
of Earth:

the long sermon
of her deserts,

the green wings
of her jungles,

the pink moths
of her cities

trembling
along the hilltops,

the thick fungus
of her buildings,

the worn brown corduroy
of her farms,

the walking symphonies
of dappled cells.

III

A waltzing iceberg
large as life,

it arrives with a shout
and will go
with a whisper,

vanish from
the fragrant isolation
of our skies,

tugged away
by a grip beyond plea,
beyond mourning,

as if it heard news
from a far country.
It will leave with its cold

gemlike pith,
a moment's gorgeous visitor,
fading.

HAWAIIAN STORMS

Do you remember that lush, dead-end road
atop Halualoa, where macadamia nuts grew
in rows tidy as a bank balance,
ring-necked pheasants barked hoarse threats
at passing dogs, and the ditches glistened with
   bougainvillea
blushing a hundred parables of twilight?

How the rain poured thick as honey,
as we parked our rented red convertible
and strolled through the downpour,
letting the sky spill over our faces.
O the sky dripped from our chins, as we tossed
a balled-up Coca-Cola can, playing catch
and singing spirituals in the rain.

It was the first day we were ourselves
together, and we sang in tune, drenched with life.
Rain and fog blued the Kona coast below
into a single long shudder; for sweet hours,
the world abandoned all its horizons.

"Listen," you said suddenly,
stopping by the barbed-wire fence
along the roadside. A deep thick flutter,
as of thunder in mud, rippled for long seconds,
then six bays raced up a distant gulley,
their tails held high in long-division signs,
their gallop rapid, muffled and deep:
hooves of panic horses.

Ghostlike, they drifted in and out of mist,
steam rising from their flanks,
their snorts small white carnations,

as they tore like summer through the heart
of the field, and earth held its breath.

Stunned by the blunt fury of their limbs,
the mud-thunder quickening, and the sky
falling thick as grain, we stood,
arms wrapped tight around each other,
while the horses pranced, then bolted away.

That night, we slept side by side, without loving,
the rain opened all its trapdoors, O the rain
fell dark as fresh violets, and I wondered how the bays
would find rest, so fearful of bright storms.
Sometimes, when you stirred, I could feel
the muffled thunder of your heart,
too troubled for sleep: hooves of panic horses.

ST. LOUIS BOTANICAL GARDENS

The orchid exhibit

In my glamorous pouch
baby kangaroos could nestle,
but I'm built to hold water,
one ladleful per bird.
Sip, friend, and travel.
Distracted by the jibbering plenty
of the jungle, *rest here*
then carry the message in my cells.

Harlots' frillies in lavender plaid,
iridescent puce, and a boa
of plashing maroon down a stem
iced with glitter. What will fetch
the silent exclamation from a bee?
Come, friend, torch your heels
with my pollen. Carry me like a rumor
through the green tides of your jungle.

The world's most pampered flower,
we are velvet paunch, we are brassy blondes.
While outside, at 35° Fahrenheit,
squirrels wait in suspense
for the headlines of spring,
and in Australia wallabies
steal the crop of winter grapes,
we're cossetted and coaxed

by servile human hands, which keep
our silk purses steamy ripe. We dine
on the equivalent of larks' tongues
and chocolate. We are free

from that slum of hummingbird and drizzle.
Why bother with a mosquito's
languid toilet? Why bother
with the pooled vulgarity of the rain?

DINNER AT THE WALDORF

Still glistening, I rush in
from the wild country of the soul,
where jungle slithers
by moonlight, natives barter
with radiant ore in tropic heat,
all death's vines hang
shimmery close, and the only way out

is when you offer me the cool perch
of your arm, nourish me
with delicacies worldless
and rare: shrimp the size
of palominos, macaroons,
the double espresso of your regard.

Unleash me, and I am an ocelot
all appetite and fur
stalking the far fields to snare game.

But now your hands are as strong
a truth as the moon, your hands
are steel ribbons hauling me back
from where it's easy to forget
one's way, or self, in the wilds
of that breathless, bud-breaking Amazon.

NIGHT LETTER TO LOREN EISELEY

All night an illness barred me
from that loam-rich sleep
we mammals are born to,
we who lie flat for eight hours
in darkness, then rise, barely rested,
for half a sun, watch color TV
because ancestors had eyes cued
to ripening fruit, laze on platforms
in the sun, and still marvel
at hand-me-down miracles like birth.

Near dawn, I took your *Immense Journey*
from the shelf, and found myself soon
with lantern-jawed humans, trapped
in the Lost Horizon of our past,
with deft orb-weavers, oracular fish,
and marsh birds that stilt
from pond to pond. Then, nodding
in ricochet delight, I feasted
on the spellbinding fruit you grew—
that way of beholding
which is a form of prayer,
and, on the still white winter morning,
knew I would carry its seeds
to an unworldly place.

Where the Sun Dines

POEMS OF AMAZONIA

IN THE RAIN FOREST

I

Dawn on the Amazon. The sun wobbles
like a thick red caramel. Among the trees,
a fidgeting chorus of bright birds squawk
anthems of love, sunlight and trouble.
Wet ropes twisting into a chirpy screech
are parakeets. Toucans yap like dogs, and hawks
blurt loud kazoos, while doves swoon and gargle.

Although complexity excites the mind,
pattern rewards it: among the tangled sheen
of roots, river bank, dense trees, I find
the shape of a tawny Indian boy, teeth filed
to piranha points, fishing in muddy shoals
beneath the sun and birds, which do not mean
to be beautiful. They cannot help themselves.

COBOCLO

(noun: an Amazonian of mixed descent)

II

Lying in the strong brown arms of your river,
while time does a shadow dance over the water,
birds call, and life clings everywhere like mist
in the great humid embrace of the jungle,
I watch you fish in tinsel light at dusk:
lifting your net like a hemp skirt stitched with lead,
you tether one end in your mouth and *hurl*
—an arcing spiderweb floats over the water
then sinks into turmoil where jaws wait.

What wonderment in the flow of the net,
its calm descent, how it vanishes in darkness
but rises again, seizing fin and mouth:
bony-tongued fish, cashew piranha,
fruit-crushing tambaki, armored catfish
whose pupils are upside-down omegas.

While sunlight makes gold foil of the river,
you lift a long glistening fish in dark hands.
A lemon-bellied bird wings low and fast,
caroling its name: *Bem ti ver! Bem ti ver!*
Water hyacinths bob with purple flowers.
The siren song of an oropendola
starts with a wet, two-stage warble—
a liquid undulating smooch, part throb,
part Moog synthesizer—and ends
with a debutante throwing kisses underwater.

Stars drift like a pack of barracudas
across the sky, and you gather your net,

guide home a canoe low-slung and tippy,
its paddle a black exclamation point
darting into the tea-stained water,
despite the six vultures in a tree on shore,
waiting like a small court of death.

AT BRAZIL,
WHERE THE SUN DINES

III

On Halloween, we drop anchor at Altar do Chão
on the Rio Tapajós, a clear-water river
so wide we cannot see the distant shore.
A white scimitar beach sweeps around a peninsula
where tiny frogs hop near the tideline,
sandstone boulders lie ribboned with lavender,
rubber trees ooze latex at recent scores,
and we build a whumping fire for a barbecue
of fish, sausage, steak, mango chutney.
A Filipino plays guitar, and the crew sing
mournful songs in Tagalog, as the sun drains
and we lie below the spasms of distant stars.

But for stingrays, there's nothing much to fear,
so, by moonlight, we snorkel round the riverbed
with lanterns, our wonder softly glowing.
Small eels slither, carving sinewy trails.
Other creatures have left hieroglyphics
in the sand, but we cannot read them
any more than the Morse code of the crickets,
the semaphore of the night owl's ears,
the wind vowels, the fluent grammar of the stars.
Submerging, I drink a mouthful of the river,
which tastes tinny and soft, as if stirred
by water hyacinths, mechanical watches and dolphins.
A stiff brown sail reels into focus:
a large clam lying on edge in the sand.
Lamp off, we see the sharp flint-like moon
twisting its bright knives through the water
and tossing onto the waves small garlands of light.

On shipboard, later, I crumble the bark
of some *casca preciosa,* fragrant relative of sassafras,
and steep it in a small pot on my bedside table,
as my thoughts begin to glide over the river
that flows in only one direction, like time,
despite its lightly feathered surface, its plumage
of small puckers, its rapids and backwaters.
Quarantined to the present, what misfit hearts we keep.
Time is the least plausible of our fictions,
and yet we dwell in it as in a house of cards.
Soon tea bouquet scents my mouth, hair, the room,
washes up over my face, and through the porthole
I watch night's crystal blackness settling in,
then lightning begin to prowl the peninsula,
as I sip the sweet violet-scented tonic,
feel an elevator drop sideways in my chest,
and drift from the river into a river of dreams.

BEIJA-FLOR

(Hummingbird)

IV

When you kiss me, moths flutter in my mouth;
when you kiss me, leaf-cutting ants lift up
their small burdens and carry them along
corridors of scent; when you kiss me,
caymans slither down wet banks in moonlight,
jaws yawning open, eyes bright red lasers;
when you kiss me, my tiny fist conceals
the bleached skull of a sloth; when you kiss me,
the waters wed in my ribs, dark and pale
rivers exchange their potions—she gives him
love's power, he gives her love's lure;
when you kiss me, my heart, surfacing, steals
a small breath like a pink river dolphin;
when you kiss me, the rain falls thick as rubber,
sunset pours molasses down my spine
and, in my hips, the green wings of the jungle flutter;
when you kiss me, blooms explode like land mines
in trees loud with monkey muttering
and the kazooistry of birds; when you kiss me,
my flesh sambas like an iguana; when you kiss me,
the river-mirror reflects an unknown land,
eyes glitter in the foliage, ships pass
like traveling miracle plays, and coca sets
brush fires in my veins; when you kiss me,
the river wraps its wet thighs around a bend;
when you kiss me, my tongue unfolds its wings
and flies through shadows as a leaf-nosed bat,
a ventriloquist of the twilight shore
which hurls its voice against the tender world
and aches to hear its echo rushing back;

when you kiss me, anthuria send up
small telescopes, the vine-clad trees wear
pantaloons, a reasonably evitable moon
rises among a signature of clouds,
the sky fills with the pandemonium
of swamp monkeys, the aerial slither
and looping confetti of butterflies;
when you kiss me, time's caravan pauses
to sip from the rich tropic of the heart,
find shade in the oasis of a touch,
bathe in Nature carnal, mute and radiant;
you find me there trembling and overawed;
for, when you kiss me, I become the all
you love: a peddler on your luminous river,
whose salted-fish are words, daughter
of a dolphin; when you kiss me, I smell
of night-blooming orchids; when you kiss me,
my mouth softens into scarlet feathers—
an ibis with curved bill and small dark smile;
when you kiss me, jaguars lope through my knees;
when you kiss me, my lips quiver like bronze
violets; oh, when you kiss me . . .

The White Lantern

POEMS OF ANTARCTICA

ANTARCTICA CONSIDERS HER
EXPLORERS

I

Brash as brash ice, they flock to me
though I chill and defy them;
keen as migrating birds they come,
all white like the kelp goose,
and too hot, too frail, too soft-skinned—
to put it bluntly, too *animal*—
for my small eternities of ice.

They come to me by water, by sled,
by sky, over seas heaving like frightened children.
I have seen them rip apart the tight skirts
of the rain, and plunge through ice packs
dense as thunder. Yet they come to me
dressed in the plumage of birds—
orange and red—like birds they nest
among twigs and sing songs,
strut, flap their arms in the cold.

They would sooner bare their souls
than their flesh, so they come to me
swathed in fur, down and leather
they strip from lesser beasts,
and walk through my crystal orchards
quilted in tight posses of life—
needing the world's full bestiary to face
my staggering chasms, my cascading glare.

They come to me during the longest night
they can find, a night elaborate and deep,
with none of the pastel preambles of twilight,
to lie long in my flesh and fill me with fire.

Bringing their starry eyes, their cunning,
their hot blood, their beautiful fever,
they pour like lava through my limbs,
pour slowly, from one shore to the other,
and leave me shaking with unearthly calm.

They are coming now—I feel their pulse
rapid as wings beating at my fingertips,
taste their salty skin, as they sweat hard
under layers of goose down and silk.
Lusty as waterfalls, tough as granite,
they have come to seize me, chaste and sparkling,
with their small arms and huge hearts,
these madmen who yearn like the sun,
torrid, molten, who mood like chameleons,
these fierce dreamers, these bright blades.

ANTARCTICA OFFERS SCOTT HER LANTERN

II

I am so cold tonight. Lend me your fever
to mull my long pastures of crumbling ice.
Warm the jagged mountains in my spine
that now shiver with cold. I will lie still as statuary.
I will hang my white lantern across your gaze
so you may see it shining, feel its sudden glow,
use it to construe the dark corners of your life.
As you wade through my snowy limbs,
I will fill you with wonder. True, I will hurl you
hard against your nerve, till your colors flare
like an aurora in the open arms of the sky.

Has the spectrum shattered across the ice?
I see you walk through blue only—
a dim, narrow band. Once fluorescent with life,
you grow faint in dismal shadows.
Your temperature has taken flight
like a small Antarctic bird and begun circling
the cliff head, climbing higher and higher.
Your fever troubles me. I am afraid
your pulse may swerve, your passion waver,
deliriums gallop through your mind
like ghost ponies, and your brave heart stumble.
Beg me once again, and I will soothe your fever.
But if I press my cold palms to your face,
you will be mine forever.

SONG OF THE CURRENT AT CAPE HORN

III

Come ride the fish-bright
   swells of my flesh
and lay-by in my limbs,
   greener than a glade.
Run aground, sailor,
   in my dark, tussocked eyes
swing round your mizzen,
   shipwreck in my thighs.

Only, come to my harbor.
   Sweet is the port air.
Time will drop its sail
   like a clipper in a lagoon.

There's a berth in my hips
   as wide as the moon,
a ribcage roomier than the sea,
   and here, awash
between outcry and the deep blue,
   my plunging heart
will fathom life from you.

KING PENGUINS

Salisbury Plain, South Georgia

IV

Carved gold in the middle of her cheeks,
her dishy commas shimmer in the sun
as she swaggers demurely, leading the boys on.
Throwing his head back, a male trumpets and raves,
and sounds like an harmonica or an oncoming train.
Her velvet commas are the hottest he's seen in days,
and her apricot bill just takes his breath away.

So, despite the rapid skuas, and the fur seals seething,
and the other avid suitors flapping and reeling,
he sidles up close and bump-herds her away
to the outskirts of the rookery for a little heavy breathing.

Her mother was right, of course:
    He'll walk all over her.

But for the moment she is Cleopatra, Marilyn,
Mata Hari all in one: dawn blooms at her throat
and the South Georgia seas, so fertile and rich,
all begin at her knees. He's not worried
if she's fit enough to raise a good brood
and outwit life's harsher dramas.
He only knows she was meant for him.
    And she has a great pair of commas.

AT BELINGSHAUSEN, THE RUSSIAN BASE, ANTARCTICA

v

Sometimes, in the long-lost continent
of an hour, my oceangoing vessels drift
back to port, their scented oils lost,
luscious cargoes turned to dust,
their hulls a pandemonium of echoes
that creak like bark ripped off a living oak.
Then, missing you, my heart recites
the full alphabet of longing, and I dream
of passion whisking us in its gleaming sleigh
across the cold flat glacier of the night
to a small dacha, where we feast like tsars:
moon on the half-shell, a side order of stars,
far from familiars, work, time or costume.
Love's mansion has so many rooms.

VI

1

On Signy Island, in the South Polar Seas,
we stole among large, addled fur seals
whose warnings gurgled like water
down a drain, as they charged and bluffed,
then climbed through dense rookeries
of chinstrap penguins
dressed and moving like Kabuki dancers,
scrawmed on hands and knees over ledges,
searching for the Antarctic prion,
a gray-white bird that sieves for krill
and nests deep within overlapping rocks.

Crouching, we could see downy fluff
and one eye, lit like polished ebony,
sparkling from a dim, slanted hole.
Bob and Peter stretched their long arms
into her den; clean up to the shoulders,
they swiveled, yearned, hung upside
down like chickadees, grasping blind.
"Pri*out*, it should be called," Bob said,
gave up at last, and the men climbed on.

Stripping down, I tilted my arm into her den,
plunged full, twisted, touched her sudden beak,
seized it fast and towed her gently out,
settled her trembling in my hand. I had never held
a bird before in the loose cage of my fingers,
and there she was: *desolata,* pale and pristine,
whose tiny beak, when it bit, focused the whole
of her feathered dream onto one sharp point.

The men laughed, as men sometimes do
at such moments. Peter measured his long arms
against mine, shoulder to shoulder.
His hands, steady as a sextant, have collared
the delicate windpipe of a petrel chick,
stopped flight with paintbrushes light as a hair,
held the squirming world in their poised grip,
while mine still tremble when lit by wonder.

The other birders teased: How could I reach
the prion that eluded both men?
Peter said: "Women are more tenacious."
And I: "Women are better at insinuation."

2

Tonight, in the narrow log-jam of my cabin,
while crash ice loudly scours the hull
and the moon hangs like a faint sword overhead,
my mind roams the cliffs riddled with prions.

Though I am weak as a breaking wave
at times, more awkward than a landing albatross,
and fumblingly ignorant of nature's ways,
my heart goes birding in all love's countries,
takes the rock paths edged with shale,
will climb up to far fields if need be,
because one never knows in what grotto
and beneath which rock lies *desolata.*

But sometimes, in my eagerness
to discover life's hidden marvels,
I reach into the tight awkward places
a man keeps to himself, and find there,
huddled under a ledge, armored by the earth,
a brilliant flutter of wings, a flash of beak.

Tugging it gently from its den, in tenderness
and passion, I forget that it must be held
like the feathered mystery it is, without crush or panic,
loose enough that it can breathe deep,
flex its huge wings, and fly free if it wants,
but snug enough that it will wish to stay.

Tales from
a Sonnetarium

OASIS

I

A kiss good-bye, I close the door, and hear
your footsteps down the hall, then fall to bed,
the galaxies in my veins still waltzing,
my skin made flawless by your perfect touch.
A moth turns its small wings at the window.
The full city moon, so buxom and bright,
astonishes the glass: somnambulisms of light
float like angels through the musky room,
across the brass bed and the pink roses,
where you felt my heart grow wild as tinder,
and set small sweet land mines in my hips.
Your face flashed semaphores of delight.
In the darkness, I read your lips with my lips.
And a sherbet moon melted on the night.

Long before we were comrades-in-arms,
we fought our wars, though we were light infantry
caught in ambushes of rage, hand-to-hand
combat, wounds that age infants overnight,
but rarely heal. Then you went off to Vietnam,
and I to a seething campus twilight.
Suppose that I had fought, like you, felt steel
blow fire through my flesh, and life's red lava
pouring out? *Killed.* Learned what terrors
I controlled, saw skies rain fire on patrol,
set loose the rats that nibble at the soul?
What different roads have led us here. Yet, sprung
from those battlefields we both remember,
we lay down our arms in love. Never surrender.

II

How like a virus entering a cell,
libertine, blasé, pollen-thighed,
you threw your coat aside
and pumped your salty cargo pell-mell
through my delicate biosphere.
In that tidal basin where life's begun,
your twin orchids blazed like suns:
white heat eclipsing but to reappear.
And how I sculled through your mind-lagoons
(vetchy, radiant, thick with fauna),
regaled by egret-flight and japonica,
deadsummer, when in arctic rooms
time rode the floe of our imaginings,
and my heart beat faster for its clipped wings.

KISMET

III

*"What can't be said can't be said,
and can't be whistled either."*

—*Wittgenstein*

Wittgenstein was wrong: when lovers kiss
they whistle into each other's mouth
a truth old and sayable as the sun,
for flesh is palace, aurora borealis,
and the world is all subtraction in the end.

The world is all subtraction in the end,
yet, in a small vaulted room at the azimuth
of desire, even our awkward numbers sum.
Love's syllogism only love can test.

But who would quarrel with its sprawling proof?
The daftest logic brings such sweet unrest.
Love speaks in tongues, its natural idiom.
Tingling, your lips drift down the xylophone
of my ribs, and I close my eyes and chime.

IV

Under the floodlight, a fawn-colored spider
I've named *Anha the aranha*
pegs out her perfect web, ten feet by six,
on a loom arching from the roof to porch rail.
By day, she shuns the zealous eyes of a bird,
but night sets her free to rig a frail quilt
between her and the blackness. She homesteads
the air with slick strands from her belly,
building a radar net all gossamer and hunch.
A folktale in outline, her guy wires
withstand the day. By nightfall, she loads them,
sliding at angle, moving right to left,
like a hand playing an auto-harp.
The moon walks her silk, the wind makes it hum.

THE LINE

V

The Line, whimsy's altar, the world unwound,
   slivered fate, footprints narrow as a name,
   streets of idleness, the ineffable outlined,
spoors down the snowy vellum of the page;

Speaking's better prank, nowhere's railing,
   the long of it made short, Mr. Bones's bones,
   tails that tattle when the rattle fails,
mitered meaning, suspenders for the cloth of gold;

Recovered falls, a short leash for doggerel,
   the cot of an idea, George Herbert's prayer,
   threads out of the maze, precious little,
overlays for a *Gray's Anatomy* of despair;

   blind rhythm's crutch, life between the margins,
   chaos aligned, where the tug of war ends.

THE WHITE HYPNOSIS

VI

of the overlapping waves, boiling surf
   into a green-gray howl,
the waves rearing up like cobras to strike,
   then sighing back from the lips of the boardwalk,
as waves, thick as rolling whales,
   spume white and roll again and spume again,
the waves' habitués watch from blanket or deck chair,
   with a patience powerful as thick green glass:
the cabaret of petticoats: the waves rolling
   without plot or purpose, as we will be in time,
without plot or purpose: which is why the gulls glide
   like a pair of brackets overhead,
and the waves run like herds of white mice
   between the hypnotic tantrums of the surf.

STILL LIFE

The bullet has almost entered the brain:
I can feel it sprint down the gun barrel,
rolling each bevel around like a hoop
on a pigslide of calibrated steel and oil.
Now it whistles free and aloft
in that ice-cold millimeter of air,
then boils as the first layer of skin
shales off like ragged leaves of soap.
The trigger's omnipresent click
makes triggers all over the body fire.
Now it tunnels through palisades,
veins, arteries, white corpuscles
red and battered as swollen ghosts,
cuts the struts on a glacial bone
jutting out like the leg of a single flamingo,
feints and draws in close for the kill,
egged on by a mouse-gray parliament of cells.

A PILOT'S PAY

My love, who rides the black flanks of the night
  on steel wings,
My love, whose sex is an inkwell, whose eyes are caged
  birds,
My love, who yawns above cities feathered with soot,
  and over jungles deadly as an arsenal,
My love, whose laugh is a peony walking a tightrope,
My love, who spins a radar net across the sky,
My love, whose hands are the fringed undulation of a hawk
  tilting calmly where only predators float,
My love, who sharpens the day on the carborundum
  of his fear,
My love, whose palms are road maps, whose lips are a
  dragonfly,
My love, who slays the wolves of inertia,
My love, who counts the loose sequins of city lights
  and the spiraling galaxies high above on the same abacus,
My love, who gallops through time and thunder,
  while clouds spill over him bags of light,
My love, who meets his enemies in sleeves of armor,
My love, whose love is a ladder of fishhooks,
My love, who finds me a wild, iridescent thing of the earth,
My love, who spreads open the loose gown of the rain
  so a wing may pass,
My love, whose feet are two panting ravens,
My love, who navigates by satellite and silo,
My love, who loves through Civil Evening Twilight,
My love, who lives by gasoline and starlight.

SONG OF THE TRILOBITE

Long before Pliocene's
celebration
of the spine,
when silver birch leaves
flickered
like tiny salmon
and grebes first hinted
at lunacy,
I paddled mud banks
ajell with bacterial slime,
hard pressed
to keep body and soul together.

But it wasn't that I
hauled genetic cargo
from the sea.
I merely bedded
the muzzy swamplands
of New York,
coining armor plate,
jointed leg,
tough, chitinous jaw
—anything to beat
extinction's warrant.

Still, the bone tumblers
ogle my chalky remains,
this herringbone shell
—wonderwork
risen out of panic.
They allude to the crab,
spider, millipede,
say *adaptive radiation*
about a common theme.

As if that explained
the papery organs within,
the crisis
that fed my opportunity.

LAMENT OF THE BANYAN TREE

How my roots fandango,
shag down
dark as anchovy fillets
gibbet-curing
in the sun
or, wind-spurred,
dicker, dodder, swoop and dodge.

Birds wheeling above
like parasols
blur
the sun's torrid obligato.
Soil humors me.
I really can't complain.

It's only that I hover
so unclad:
vines at peril,
flighty, without hitch.

I absorb what I can,
but rarely do my pendent shoots
touch down,
and what misery
when they nod
an inch
that might as well be an ocean
from pay dirt, and I crane
at my wit's end,
unable to connect.

Spine anchored
in the plenary dust,
I could abide the wind

fitfully orphic
and hushed-up,
tolerate drab insects
needling my bark,
even brook
that indecent commotion
within me
that every winter renews.

But now and then, stateless
after a savage peace,
my dozy tendrils
quiver and flinch.
The soil begins to shudder.
I feel an urgent tugging at my cuff,
sudden, miraculous,
and know a root any moment
will come alive, steeled
by that slender, radical grip.

POEM IN WINTER

I

These lines
only a few
heartbeats wide,
a gentle palpitation
I send you.

For, like Lady Macbeth,
I have time
on my hands.
The snow is blowing
sideways: a hard white
artillery.

You are somewhere
in the open prison
of your city,
living long and fast,
a blue iris
in a vase,
stiff with your flow,
tense and electric.

And I am on ice.
The sun has set
like a thin yellow liquid
draining out,
and I need you
to redden
my dumb white bones
from within, manhandle
each rib again.

II

You are making
fade away jump shots
in my dreams.
They are slow-motion,
gorgeous, strained,
and uprushing.
The ball arcs
with a salmon's purpose,
and you fall back
as if to blazing
water, my arms.

Like the stars,
I am frantic tonight.
My hands
are two clenched
fortune cookies.
Inside, the message
reads:
Only the kidnapped life
is worth living.

III

Love, do with me
what summer does
in the willows.

CAMPUS CEMETERY

Ruminant tonight,
I explored a graveyard
terracing downhill
from the founder's old place,
ducked my head
as I strolled
among the grasping
conifers, and was struck
by the pale candor
of each slab:
MOTHER FATHER LOUISE RICHARD
planted a jump apart,
steppingstones
leading through shallow grass
to greener waters.

My student, John,
the naturalist, came too,
and, meandering steeply,
my hand a falcon
perching on his arm,
he showed me
where mausoleums lie
like prairie sod houses,
some topped with obelisks,
others dwarfing
the spirits they entomb,
but all macabre:
stripes of pink, buff
and black; keystones
bold as ciphers;
vetch delving obsessively
into brick; ivy tangled
like windblown hair.

In one shrine
nine vaults lay open
to view,
three of them full,
the others waiting.
Small bats flew,
shuttlecocks among the branches.
But John was study-bent,
gauging yew spore's fabric
between his fingers,
plucking the wraithlike stem
of a bluebell,
browsing a slim tree
pruned to bush wide.
"Maple," he said,
haunted by the Knowable,
and eased bud layers back
to show me fissure and fold,
his wonder a lamp
in the wolflike shadows.

I meant to pry the gloom
open, too, like John,
be lark-tongued and breezy
but my eyes kept dropping
to that never-blooming garden
set row after row,
till my ribcage mumbled
like a gourd,
and I was all audience
to the silent undoing.

LETTER TO WALLACE STEVENS

Heartless in a Hartford long dissolved,
    you were the axis
        of my revolving world

when, at nineteen, I desired your gift
    and Dylan Thomas's:
        his voluptuousness of mind,
            your sensuous rigor.

I didn't know then that Art
    is the best one rises to,
        a momentary privilege.

I didn't know that bad men
    could write good poems,
        be spiteful to all,

cruel to their children,
    but wholly compassionate
        to ideal compassion.

Rude, icy, alert to advantage,
    rapt but condescending,
        terrified to be cornered
            into a friendship,

you knew the dollar each lily concealed
    and fantasized a Paris
        laminated by distance,

whose essence you took
    in strong, cunning draughts.
        Few speak well of you,
            the glacial man in the baggy suit.

The new biography makes me a fortuneteller
in reverse. I watch you weaken
in your garden robust with peonies

where you ushered in the world
and escaped your wife (whose face, on the liberty dime,
sat in your pants pocket all day).

But your poems, what madrigals,
canny and luscious, in which the Sinbads
of thought wear twirling knives,

and you steer by the polestar
of your own invention. Your nomadic eye
roamed the seven seas
of the seven senses.

By heart, and by law,
you could toss a bucketful of light
onto any dim object, make ideas fluoresce,

and stain the willows with a glance.
You named the chaos.
You could dry out the sun.

I wish you'd reveled in the deserts—
Egypt, Africa, the Southwest—
but it wasn't your fault

that world is ampler than you knew.
Anyway, a coral key can be played
to the absolute,

and desert bluffs arrive by ship in New England,
where tide can be touched
and night is a leopard.

VISITING PROFESSORS

We live in a monsoon of steel,
someone else's city,
in two residential hotels across town.

Mafiosi, courtesans, shut-ins, and us.
Crockery's laid on. All mod cons.
There are shops downstairs, a laundry and spa.
Valets park our cars.

And we furnish our vacant, over-lit rooms
with pylons of friendly books,
cheap flowers in a tumbler, and postcards
dwarfed by the white tundra of the walls.

We live high above the cobblestone
and the lovers dodging traffic hand in hand
as they whip across the street,
laughing, alight with their deep, open kisses.

We live below the five stars
of Pitt's Cathedral: a neon Pleiades,
and the sole constellation

when ground light blurs a million suns
and incoming jets drift pterodactyl slow
minute by fossil minute overhead.
They remind you of dining cars
in paintings by Hopper.

We live in a river delta
whose only roads lead away, through tubes
and over a ribcage of bridges.

In the morning, Christ floats
upon the water, then steel dross
and the rest of the city follow.

We live in the outback of our art,
in the ground zero of a visiting term,
cramming time's empty rooms
with bric-a-brac that don't match:
B-movies, pizza parties, civil teas with deans,
public readings, ballroom dancing at HoJo's.

We accept every last invitation
to drink beer out of fridge or bartap,
but leave early

to straight vodka and rum,
Thelma Ritter and Raymond Massey
on *The Late Show,* in our twin sarcophagi
until the test patterns of dawn.

We live in the august relief
of each other, wit galloping
and giddy when we meet.

We chum up for movies, chores and museums,
killing time with a tact
so gallant it could derange,
then hurry home to call our loved ones
as soon as the rates change.

AIR SHOW IN BARBADOS

How could it ever end,
his silvery jet blades
slicing the day open
like the carcass
of a wide blue animal?

The fire he steals
begins and ends with him,
as migrated wonder,
and he chews on that thrill
like the raw meat it is,

though fear's a lame buck
flung over his shoulder,
antlers probing deep.

"Kick the tire, light the fire,
and go!" he says,
climbing into an isolation
booth where he lusts
for precision.

Muscle is out of date.
When he asks the computer
to bankroll a loop,
he is six again, playing
Simon Sez. *Barrel roll?*
he asks with the touch
of a dragonfly
landing on the console,

then accuses a button
with one finger,
and the F-15 veers

through turns at 7 g's,
wave-lap to stratosphere
in eight seconds,
his G-suit puffs hard
to full leg, full belly,
squeezing toward a heart
already at its limit
able only to pump blood
to the center of his eyes.

Panorama fades:
he sees the world through a small tube:
as he angles straight up
at glass-shattering speed
from deep sea
to the Barbados of dollar
and shack-talk
and cinderella liberty
and bathers recently amazed
by jockeys swimming
thoroughbreds out to the reef.

A wasp, his heartbeat
stings in his chest.
But it's all so abstract
now: the idea of flight
he rolls around his tongue,

his jet the loudest word
the air speaks,
sound an erupting mumble
that wells
up in his mind,
flits to his finger,
then zooms toward a future
he explodes with a shout.

At the Hilton pool, later,
servicemen flirt
and play water games.
They address him as "Killer"
and beg him to join in.
But he stands up to his waist
in a remote corner,
short, wiry, and silent,
watching clouds stalk
the sky-blue water,
his mind an abacus
cleared after a large sum.

THE MANURE GATHERERS

Steam rises from manure-and-straw
   heaped on cold stone between the stalls,
     and steam from the men
    whose breath ghosts the air
as they pitch forkfuls at the gaping truck.

An impressionist would make guile
  of this: brown, flaxen and gold;
     round and angular;
    the men in gray jumpsuits stretching
and bending; the sunlight lamé of wet straw.

   Minded narrowly in wooden stalls,
twelve horses stretch black rubber anuses
     to dump what the men
    will cart away.
Renewal is the profit and drudgery of their chore.

I watch the younger man sling manure
    overhead with a curt flick-of-the-wrist,
      his pale lashes dusted
     with paler flecks, as farmer's ore rains
onto the truck, and he whistles up an orient of light.

AT WALT WHITMAN'S BIRTHPLACE,

Huntington, Long Island

At night before the dark swells of sleep,
Walt, I think of your strong arms

that embrace whole cities, vast membranes
of streetlamp and neon, lit by the inner electric

of a million souls, where brewery workers
bet the Redbirds for the play-offs,

dirt farmers fight the locust of hard laws,
and adolescent boys, all decibel and testosterone,

dream of rapture in shiny cars. I think how your limbs,
tattooed with words, enthrall shopgirls

learning about the new deal at night school,
and bodybuilders whose flesh has stopped at midboil,

people who will one day betray their dreams,
and people who have not forgotten how to wish,

stockbrokers and deckhands and tailors and dancers,
all working in throbbing honeycombs of light,

despite the silent metronomes inside.
Yours is the counterpoint that wakes them from sleep;

yours the spark that sets brushfires in their veins,
in the skyscrapers and row houses and tenements

and lofts where, at dusk, whole passages of light
just vanish into time. You take me to their outposts,

crackling with sweat, my curiosity buoyant
as I count the marvels, as I gather my wits.

On a bench in your yard, while a sweat bee licks
beads from my leg, I dream of your radiant white fever

jetting into me, until my backbone lunges—
a mountain range; my hips quiver wide—a Mercator projection;

worlds career on my tongue with subways,
politics, waterfalls, county fairs,

and, in an opera athletic as the land,
I drink from your source and swell large as life.

IN THE GREEN PURSE OF THE YARD
THIS LOOSE RED CHANGE

Crouched over flat leaves
which parasol the fruit,
I slide a finger deep
and roll a fat wild strawberry
along the vine, plucking it.

Though pinprick seeded,
some berries are still white.
But others dangle like miniature organs
—hearts, lungs, testes.

A squirrel joins us to feed
with the lumbering giants
who stalk nothing
and laze on platforms in the sun.

We alone keep the short-tempered wrens at bay.
Flying high to drop hard,
needle beak set for stabbing,
they vex the squirrels across the yard,
jeering and scolding.

When we stroll down to their nest
at eye level in the hickory,
they sit trigger-happy on a branch
and damn us till they're hoarse,
while squirrels boldly dare the open grass.

Ever since we judged it okay
to be scarecrows, small lives have come
to forage at our heels:
rabbits, birds, squirrels,
ground-hiving bees, ants and aphids,

daddy-longlegs whose bodies are mere buttons,
and other bugs too tiny and strange to name.

And each time we feel the centuries
slough off, the yard green up,
our brows get lower,
no rip-roaring born-again pitch,
just a quiet throb about lidless creation
and how the body remembers
what the mind forgets:
in summer's hot lull,
the gift of being ancient.

LADY CANUTE

I guess it will have to be enough
just watching the ticker-tape river,

whose sum is never in, tally light
through its sulky brown waters.

If the winds won't catechize me
in any grass-roots religion,

I'll have to do the best I can:
justify my margins, hem my desires,

wade deeper into the cosmic overwhelm,
the gladiatorial mayhem that frames us.

And it will have to be enough
that a pheasant barks hoarse threats

at a neighbor's dog, enough to hear
seedpods clatter like tiny gourds,

enough learning the habits
of the peppermint starfish.

If mum's the word, faith lies
in the details: the semaphores of flight,

the Morse codes of the heart.
It will have to be enough

to build a congregation of poems
from what is shrouded from view

and what is blooming before us,
enough just knowing the moths at twilight—

the pink wings of the city—will tremble
if I bid the waters advance.

OPENING THE LOCKET

Each night you ask about the view
from my window: the rusty U.S. Steel building
with honeycombs of thick, spreadable light,
the river wind-creased to a single
brown shudder, whose bottomless sucking
and drawing terrifies you, as love does.

Me it liberates. The river, I mean.
I know the roll of those dark wet hips
can bring a rich commotion to the numbest fields.

I tell you I woke to a blizzard today,
and thought at first I was in hospital,
the windows were so abracadabra white,
and how under hypnosis once I remembered
waking on my mother's chest in a white room.

But I tell you many views late at night,
by telephone's filamental grace, by the wire
between the two tin cans of our hearts.

Still, you will not come over. The river, you see.
The shadow egrets flying low
over fluorescent water, with glitter knives
and tense ambiguous wings.

GRAND CANYON

Geologic
in their repose,
memories lie
carameled by sunlight,

and captive
as the river
far below
the shale blossoms
of canyon wall,

each with cutting edge
and sandy flux,
each
the hem and panorama
for the next,

laid out
like so many bolts
of light fabric,
once ocean
and lava, once
lightning and fossil.

How regular,
explicable,
even dull
was the frenzy
when ruts glistened
and flooded,
pinnacles jutted up,
continents gave way,

and tawny limbs
of earth
crashed together
and held.

Now the emptiness
is larger
than anything
that defines it.

Larger
than the tantrums
of shadow and heat.

Larger
than the other canyons
whose sunlight
is image,
whose rivers
are misgiving,

in which donkeys
also walk
slender pathways
to the floor,

despite the froth
of the rapids,
despite the ancient hurling
which set all
in motion,

despite the oily black
refulgence
of the birds,
whose open wings
hold nothing,

despite the sunlight
swarming
across the valley,

an immaculate crimson
unforgettable
in the stale glare
of reflection.

LETTER OF RETAINER

for Morton Janklow

1

Dear Mort,
　(my fine agent
whose name means death),

Your retainer letter
arrived today
full of sweet plunder,

We accept this engagement

poignantly brave
and sharp as beryllium,
as if it came straight
from the agencies of summer

about my *disposition* and *tie up rights.*

How I wish
you could negotiate so well
for me with Life,

argue that I *commit sums,*

not crimes, parlay
with the whole bustling
sense-luscious ferment of it

whose *gross proceeds* we retain

only breath by breath,
in moments wide and airy as soufflé,
or lean as the appetite
of a fly, that *ent-*
ity who in midair marries and dies.

Plead like radium.
Be firm or coquettish,
be a one-man crowd,

so I may *disclose existence*

when able, if allowed.

2

The heart was made to stammer.
How I wish it weren't so.
By moonlight, even the stars
have a grammar. Before we are
deleted from these paragraphs of snow,
   I'd hold you

harmless from and against all losses

if I could,
but Earth is unforgiving.

In the samovars of night,
where all love's litanies repeat,
when grounds settle
and the time is right
we brew hope
like a small fluid contract.
   So, if you wish,

we'll *set forth* upon an *understanding,*

that far rich wild trip
so dangerous to complete
which, in the suburbs of a glance,
on any avenue, begins in risk,
where all best journeys start,
with the half-lit hieroglyphics
   of the heart.

COME PICNIC ON MARS

for Zoë, age 5

On a distant glad November,
when our hearts are running high,
and the dreambats all have vanished
into the limestone of the sky,
why don't we take a fiery stroll
straight up to Mars? Just you and I.

We will pack a mental picnic
for years before we go.
Some will say the sky's the limit,
but we will answer: No,
the mind was made to travel.
So, too, indentured hearts,
and knitted fears unravel
with adventure in the dark.

A world of blues will slowly dwindle,
as Mars glows round the bend;
the differences that blind us
will bind us in the end,
for wonder is the chorus
that makes us all a choir,
and time will not forgive us
if, slug-a-beds, we lie
fat and bored and cranky
in our hammock in the sky.

So, come and take the waters
that jet across the seas
that lie between the planets
we crawl to on metal knees.
Oh! when we arrive, what fancy stuff

we'll see: the swooning sands of *Paradise*,
dust-devils, a volcanic sea.
Then, when twilight falls, by double moon,
we'll feast on ra-
ta-
touille!

SOFT LENS

Water held by a curve,
it bridges the invisible
oceans of light
with a single continent,

is fragile as dust,
yet anchors
the Mayan profile of the moon
among night-swarming clouds.

By morning, the autumn leaves
are pinned out against the sky
with a surgeon's cunning,

and, high across the blue petition
of the day, three jets
countersign in flowing script.

It was always there,
the flaky bark of the sycamore,
in whose high pouch
a squirrel finds lodging,

despite my patrol
at an office window nearby.
The storm cloud of black hair
won't frighten it,

but possibly the carnivorous red
of the mouth, and surely the eyes,
bright purple now
clear up to the brows,

the eyes corrected
"past infinity," the doctor said,
possibly the vivisecting stares
of a woman who, at night,

will remove her tiny pond
with such sadness,
and submerge herself
in the monotone of sleep

for a soon moment
until the new world wakes
and, once again, she basks
in her optical Riviera.

PUMPING IRON

She doesn't want
the bunchy look
of male lifters:
torso an unyielding love knot,
arms hard at mid-boil.
Doesn't want
the dancing bicepses
of pros.
Just to run her flesh
up the flagpole
of her body,
to pull her roaming flab
into tighter cascades,
machete a waist
through the jungle
of her hips,
a trim waist
two hands might grip
as a bouquet.

HIGH-ALTITUDE KNITTING

I can't account for the angels.

But I no longer drop stitches
at altitude, over rivers of sand,
where I float calm at 37,000 feet
("37 angels," the test pilots say),
and do women's work old as women's work:
knit mauve pastels from two sticks
and two stitches, while mountains
creep below like crocodiles.

Dotted with scrub, the Santa Catalinas
pinken to a desert, in whose cacti
I've seen elf owls roosting,
their downy feathers angelic
among the rude spines.
Then we become the hour hand
over clock-faced pastures,
and desert turns to a flight of mesas.

The trick is not to unravel
while knitting at altitude
the invisible knots
of the visible world,
just because virus and mountain range
look the same, jag for jag,
in long and short views,
especially from the perspective
of angels, or ever stop searching
for time and the marvel
among the green sundials
of Kansas grain.

ELEGY FOR *CHALLENGER*

Wind-walkers,
how we envied you

riding a golden plume
on a glitter-mad trajectory

to watch Earth roll
her blooming hips below

and scout the shores
of still unnamed seas.

You were the Balboas
we longed to be,

all star-spangled grin,
upbeat and eager,

a nation's cameo.
When the sun went out

and you blew into your shadow,
horrors clanged

like falling bells.

You orbit our thoughts now
as last we saw you:

boarding a shuttle bound
out of this world,

quivering with thrill,
deadset, but tingling

to pitch an outpost
in our wilderness of doubt,

and climb that old ladder
whose rungs lead only higher.

We still dream your dream,
though we taste your fire.

CONFESSION

You slept
like a shaggy bison,
so I sized up your carcass
and random limbs,
ran an eye down
your cartilaginous spine.

I guessed at your waist
—where basin capsized
in a plexus
of unpronounceable bones.

At your shoulder,
I slalomed two fingers
down your side,
scaled a spade-shaped rump,
and grappled with
flimsy, triangular feet.

I sifted through
blood and cell palisades
under the skin,
raced corpuscles
in your arteries,
crammed bronchial sacs
into the lungs,
slid the liver into its slot.

I wedged the heart
below the sternum
in a cobweb of meat,
and even found a spot
for the adenoids.

However, I did have to pry
the gall bladder loose,
and the pancreas,
like the ileum,
was never sorted out.

Then I refereed
your cells' mitosis,
and the ack-ack-ack-ack
of your synapses firing.

At last, I snapped your chromosomes
like a set of reins,
carved my initials on your DNA,
short-circuited your electrolytes,
and marinated your body
in a beaker of night.

PORTRAIT WITHOUT POSE

for William Gass

1

Was that the dream, the birds clubbing up
in the trees? This vigil beside a lagoon of stars

as night pools dank and luminous?
The timberline pines all point upward

and the eye flows from ground to treetop,
then pauses . . . what a long leap into the sky.

But so easy, a voice like falling leaves
whispers, *so easy, just lean and let go.*

2

When I think of the dream, I think of days
like this one, when heat shimmer

over the trapped lucidity of the pool
is more august and certain than any creed.

Should I believe in the capital of Poland
or in these lozenges of light?

Which is irrefutable, Work = Energy × Distance
or these lozenges of light?

Which testimony is older, which temper would you harness,
what rapture is steeper

than these lozenges of light, in which all
the lost logarithms of the sun vibrate?

3

Was that the dream, any late afternoon,
when Japanese beetles couple

on the grape leaves, and the crows sound
like they're choking in the trees?

Then a milt of stars vented across the night,
a dribble from some early rage of the Universe

whose sunglow tantrum became wheat, became blood.
John Clare used to go out looking for the horizon,

where sunlight walked a tightrope
and the air was thin as a razor. I have found it

in the savory curve of this summer day.

4

When I think of the dream, I marvel
at the cell-by-cell furnace of a man

who can strike the flint in my hips
to a self-quenching flame,

the genteel treacheries of the flesh,
all the daily acts of quiet terror

an engaged heart defines. We dip into our wells
and churn up slaggy water, then search

our reflection in each other:
the hallucination of a face bone,

the red benediction of blood below the surface,
the sweet penitentiary of the body

whose bones we grip from within,
crying our innocence, begging for release.

His touch makes sound leap from my skin,
as he mulls the cool, flowing cider of my limbs.

The steam that rises has syntax,
he sends words down my spine.

5

Was that the dream, then, a man
who welds your body to his with a look?

He walks across the room. Around his neck
hangs the amulet of your desire.

He has an average build and an average face,
but his hand is large enough

to hold a live, beating heart.
Was that the dream, the banana republic of love,

where petty tyrants sweep one away
by nightfall for some gentle terror?

6

When I think of the dream
that could stay a devout watcher,

rifle loaded, in the duck shoot
of self-esteem, waiting

for one's own dazzling array to ambush,
I think of apple trees

so deformed in the cold months,
wearing Halloween masks, limbs hunched and gnarled.

You marvel blossom could irrupt,
let alone ripe fruit. I think of athletes

blowing across the grass like seeds,
anonymous, possessive, able to hold ground,

but yielding fully to each sway
in the thin harmonies of motion.

7

The invisible line of a fisherman
gesturing toward the surf—Was that the dream?

A roux of fish eggs pearled among seaweed—
Was that the dream?

The stampede of birds and mice
pumping their white forevers—Was that the dream?

The hockey goalie, falling on his knees
to propose to the goal—Was that the dream?

Castles of desire set in a kingdom
of disappointment—Was that the dream?

A code whistled underwater—
Was that the dream?

A mind that whirrs while the world inters—
Was that the dream?

8

When I think about the dream
that began with outcry and will end

with the cold mummery of bare bones,
I fix on the brown bark of shag hickories,

the sultry drawl that's summer heat,
and all the innuendos of bird and light

that make a mental breeze in the weather
of one's life, where a mass murderer

is far more explicable than a tree.
But was that the dream—shimmery patterns

in the heart's pulsarium, like constellations
tumbling from no height to no depth?

NUCLEAR WINTER

I

People with souls
luminous as watch dials
are talking about
    winter,

when the sun is white cotton
in a perishable sky,
dust clouds thicken
over the earth, water sours,
and plants forget how to green,
when summer begins at 20° below,
and then the seasons fail
all living things.

II

Moments ago, we were speechless
    shadows on the savanna,
foragers and hunters of small game.
We were tamers of wild beasts,
builders of cities.

With dreams dark and lusty as roans,
    we raised families
amid the opera of fall leaves,
and below the deep blue baritone
    of the summer sky.

Moments ago, we magicians
used fabulous machines
to shove our bodies skyward
and around the whole planet,

in wires, in lights, in pulses,
   incomparable.

III

O my planet,
where I have lingered
with the simple daily marvels
of egg and leaf,
where I have tried to be
a modest and able watcher of the skies,
and of the Earth
whose green anthem I love,
you are captained
by madmen and bullies
you do not deserve.

O my planet,
grass luscious with all
the adages of summer,
we have forgotten
that you are fragile and soft-petaled
or we are lost,

forgotten that you are all
green fugues
in a solar opus,
where shrimp and polar bear
must spawn,
or we are lost,

forgotten how many footfalls
from the cave
we have toddled,

how deftly we must pad
the catwalk of our desire,
or we are lost.

IV

Moments ago, we were veldt-walkers
forged by curiosity.
How have we come to be
exterminating angels?

For almost half my lifespan
I have lived on this planet,
but I still do not understand
the wicked beauty of the atom,
or the Easter Island of the heart.

But I understand winter.

V

In the stormwatch
for upstate New York,
a gray drizzle is falling
straight down,
stagnant, quiet, as if forever.
The deer, who leapt fences
into our yard
to savor summer apples
still sweet under the snow,
have not come for days.
Paul is freeing the windsock,
twisted and crazy
from an impetuous gale.
Indoors, I have turned the lily
round once again,

because it cannot find
an angle on the sun.
In each of us
a live siren has begun
wailing,
but we are small
radiant forms
in a vast white madness.

FRENCH FRIGATE SHOALS

When morning began blueing up the ocean,
I toured the atoll in an orange whaler,
searching each storm-fretted islet for seals.
The sun shone through washed-up fishing floats—
glass balls trembling with auroras,
and I thought of your heart, so buoyant and bright,
sowing illumination in wintry seas.

At last, sun-raw and tried, I ran
the steep swells home, and lashed the boat
bow and stern to a dock, where it shimmied,
swayed, leapt full against the planks.
And I thought of your hands, strong as hawsers,
harboring me when currents rage.

At sundown, a host of angel-bright terns
stabbed the full moon with their beaks,
and white berries tumbled
through the rich pantry of the sky—
some would call them stars.

Then night poured India ink into the sea,
a thousand wedge-footed shearwaters
began moaning in unison like orgasmic women;
a ghost walking between horizons
left silver footprints across the water,
and a dozen monk seals, snoring on the beach,
dreamt their ancient dreams.

As I lay abed, lights out, developing the day,
a tern hovered at my open window
where the wind spoke fast furious syllables,
and I thought of your eyes, exact as compass needles.
I listened for the sifting pebbles of your voice.

Then I called to you with a silent whistling,
the way a women calls a Silkie to her bed.
Half man, half ocean, loyal as the moon,
waltzing through worlds of land, magic
and myth, trailing the fluorescent fires of the sea,
he yields to her like a breaking wave.

Our flesh hot as oil lamps, swinging
and swinging, on an oceangoing vessel
whose scuttlebutt is passion, we'd find time
tilting free from the oarlocks of each day,
and lose track of infinity in a passing moment.

On your chest, I'd apply an invisible tattoo
so bold your ribs quiver; limned by hand,
it would last forever, and contain all
the human sagas in the many-sabled night.
Whenever you opened your shirt, you would see
caravans, cities, a backbone of light.

We would lie on coral sand, below sugary stars,
watching Cassiopeia mount her throne
and the Great Bear wash its paws in the South.
I would say, "I have a secret to tell you."
And, folding me in your arms, boyish and sly,
you would answer: "Whisper it into my mouth."

THE ENABLER

I

Because we're neighbors on this light-flecked street,
I see a parade of cars in your driveway,
left one by one under the pine, whose cones
litter the ground now like soft hand grenades,
charged with bloom, on a bed of yellow needles.

All day, new members of a shy brigade
I seldom see and never meet, in haste,
climb down to the foxhole of your office
lodged at the azimuth of their unrest—
above the ground, but just below the street.

Sun-struck, their cars blaze like suits of armor.
Or, cloudy days, glow dull as Etruscan mirrors.
Sometimes one waits like a carapace
for the lidless sorrow it conveyed. It's then
my quick heart grows heavy as pewter.

They are fitful or vexed, hostile or wan;
they hear time bombs, they are seeking alms;
they have drunk the long cold gin of self-hate,
found marriage a cang, loved a mirage,
dug toll roads; they are afflicted with themselves.

II

9:00 A.M.: A woman without her gravity boots
leaves the penitentiary of her car
and, too faint, too light to bear pain's cargo,
floats down the steps, skids wild into your office,
suspended. You anchor her to earth.

1:00 P.M.: A man tells you his dream
of trees dark as arrowheads, hills spotted
like fawns, geese flying—a flutter of wings.
He takes aim. Fires. The target bursts in midair.
Bloodied, he finds himself in the cross-hairs.

5:00 P.M.: A woman with burnt memories
spills cinders from her mouth, setting the rug
on fire. She finds the past pure mercury—
a puzzle to grasp. With eyes like bright ovens,
she tells you everything she knows.

III

Nomads gripping an abacus of despair,
they engage you to ford plunging rivers
and cross the starless wilderness. Their lives
are dreams whose contents you make visible.
You lead them to the fountains of innocence.

I know these things as I know the dwarf phlox
by your driveway, that started summer
twisted in blood-dark knots, but bloomed last week,
despite the cold calmatives of autumn,
to roaring pink petals and a luminous heart.

I know these things as I know your quaking
aspens and your bittersweet, on icy days
when steam sighs underfoot, lips blue with cold,
and I come to you, shivering, hands cupped
around the brazier of my small, damp soul.

Selected Poems

FROM

The Planets:

A Cosmic Pastoral

(1976)

IX WHEN YOU TAKE ME FROM THIS GOOD RICH SOIL

from *Earth*

When you take me from this good rich soil
to slaughter in your heavenly shambles,
rattle my bone-house until the spirit breaks;

no heart of mine will scurry at your call
to lie blank as a slug in the ground where
my hips once rocked and my long legs willowed.

No heaven could please me as my lover
does, nor match the bonfire his incendiary eyes
spark from dead-coal through my body's cabin.

When, deep in the cathedral of my ribs,
love rings like a chant, I need no heaven.
Though you take me from this good rich soil,

where I grew like a spore in your wily heat,
rattle my bone-house until the spirit breaks;
my banquet senses are rowdy guests to keep,

and will not retire meekly with the host.
When, midwinter at the gorge, I saw
pigeons huddling like Cro-Magnon families,

no seraphic vision could have thrilled me more.
When you take me from this good rich soil,
and my heart tumbles like the chambers

of a gun to leave life's royal sweat
for your numb peace, I'll be dragging at Earth
with each cell's tiny ache, so you must
rattle my bone-house until the spirit breaks.

VIII FULL MOON

from *Earth*

Vampiric black ether
gnawed it last month: sickle, kayak, udder, wormy peach.
Then it grew
a bull's face and floret of cauliflower, turned polar-white
on its own
stark dawn. Tonight it's whole as wheat and cartoon-round,
a ball of sump

that swills water and makes babies drop. Look, I can push in
a floury thumbprint
and, everywhere, women will drain white as shallots, hemorrhage
in their vents
and fizzle off like gas. (I think of the stars as a million
gray cataracts.
It leaves me hanging by my eyeteeth, but it leaves me hanging.)

And now that
dazzling keyhole they call a moon turns out frigid as a bat,
a slab
of scar tissue good for nothing but plant food—better than
horsemeat,
but not so cheap, say, as dung. That marbly carcass.
I wanted

something to conjure with, not magnetic sudd. Even so,
I guess
they'll strip-mine it clean as a wiffle ball, leave it
derelict—
a drafty celestial rind. I just can't get over
so round
a monstrosity. Imagine something that big being dead.

DIFFRACTION

for Carl Sagan

When Carl tells me it's *Rayleigh scattering*
that makes blue light, canting off molecular

grit, go slowgait through the airy jell, subdued,
and outlying mountains look swarthy, or wheat

blaze tawny-rose in the 8:00 sun, how I envy
his light touch on Earth's magnetic bridle.

Knee-deep in the cosmic overwhelm, I'm stricken
by the ricochet wonder of it all: the plain

everythingness of everything, in cahoots
with the everythingness of everything else.

The second pair of pants in my genetic suit
held no whys and wherefores, no clement unity,

no federation of water flea and Magellanic Cloud.
Mathematics is a language I don't speak.

I can't unveil the sun's ricy complexion, really
fathom Vela-X ticking like a clock, track comets

on the run through hyperbola, parabola or ellipse.
I'm bone-deaf to cloud-chamber music.

When Carl tells me it's *Rayleigh scattering*
that azures the sky or unpuzzles rainbow-

grinding weather, I envy his firm grip
on a world where I think not as a thinker

thinks, but as light engrossed in every object:
a doting consciousness among alien forms.

I only know, one rural twilight, when wheat
blazed like ambergris and a chicory sun

haggled with a black sky, for a moment
all the blues of the world scattered;

my ribcage sprang open like calipers, and,
in their widening compass, nothing lacked.

CAPE CANAVERAL

Miles beyond the inlet
crazed with pelicans
and the putty-blue churning
of the Banana River,
an iron thatch
stood its ground
like a sentinel,
gripping the stiletto
rocket to its heart.

The sky put on a summer frock.
Cloudbanks piled
like a Creation scene,
dwarfing all
but a ghostly trail
embossed on the gravelpath
below (like the tread
of some rampaging mammoth)
where, earlier,
a tons-heavy slug
creaked its towering heft
along, to ferry
the *Viking* craft upright.

We glued our hopes
to that apricot *whoosh*
billowing across the launch pad
in spasms, like the rippling
quarters of a palomino,
and now outbleaching
the macaroon sun,
as a million pounds of thrust
paused
a moment

on a silver haunch,
and then the bedlam clouds let rip.

Gnats capered everywhere
in the marshland viewing site,
driven from their quiddities
by the clamor
pealing tindery to world's-end.
And how I envied
the wheat-colored moths
flitting about in a spry tizzy,
blind to that rising
persuasion called flight
groaning on a tower downwind.

I knew surf-jockeys
rode their rollercoaster sea
on this ordinary day
in an ordinary August;
couples huddled on beachtowels
as if on loveseats.
Perhaps they'd see
an odd blaze far off,
Viking slide into the air
like a flint into water.

I was thinking of vigils:
radar hubs
following the craft
like sunflowers,
tracking dishes worldwide
now and again
rolling their heads
as if somehow
to relieve the tension,
how we'd gathered

on these Floridian bogs
to affirm the sanctity of Life
(no matter how or where
it happens), and be drawn,
like the obelisk we launch,
that much nearer the infinite,

when iron struts
blew over the launch pad
like newspapers,
and shock waves rolled out,
pounding, pounding
their giant fists.
My highflying pulse
dove headlong,
and then, like a cagebird
whose time was due,
my heart lifted off
into the breathtaking blue.

THE OTHER NIGHT (COMET KOHOUTEK)

Last night, while
cabbage stuffed with
brown sugar, meat and
raisins was baking in the
oven, and my potted holly,
dying leafmeal from red-spider,
basked in its antidote Malathion,
I stepped outside to watch Kohoutek
passing its dromedary core through the
eye of a galaxy. But only found a white
blur catnapping under Venus: gauzy, dis-
solute, and bobtailed as a Manx.

Pent-up in that endless coliseum of stars,
the moon was fuller than any Protestant
had a right to be. And I said: Moon,
if you've got any pull up there, bring me
a sun-grazing comet, its long hair swept
back by the solar wind, in its mouth a dollop
of primordial sputum. A dozing iceberg,
in whose coma Ur-elements collide.
Give me a thrill from that petrified seed.

Mars was a stoplight in the north sky,
the only real meat on the night's black
bones. And I said: Mars, why be parsimonious?
You've got a million tricks stashed
in your orbital backhills: chicory suns
bobbing in viridian lagoons; quasars dwindling
near the speed of light; pinwheel, dumbbell,
and impacted galaxies; epileptic nuclei
a mile long; vampiric moons; dicotyledon suns;
whorling dustbowls of umbilical snow; Milky Ways
that, on the slant, look like freshly fed pythons.

Sirius began to stammer overhead, jittery
as a blue-assed fly. And I said:
All right, then, let's put our cards
on the table. I've never quite believed
that rumor of cohesive unity, in which all
things participate and adhere. Never felt part
of that black long-winded millennium
which, I'm told, is expanding with unhindered
clarity. Never could accept the extortionist
behavior of germs as part of some ebullient
inhuman will whose codicil's unknown.
And in this fleshy vellum, which I assume
to be mortal (there being no news flash
to the contrary), my mind can't conceive of
what it can't conceive of. I've got a brain
all dressed up and no place to go. Why don't you
hatch me a dream from that frogspawn cloud
of comets ambling up and down the carborundum
sky, whose sudsy white nougats of dust and ice
may be the only spirits in a lidless night.

from *Mercury*

                                    Hobnobbing
around the Mercurian noon, with only a thin
whiskey-colored veil
to waylay it,
the Sun must burn carte blanche in the sky,
                        growing white-hot
                            and even larger
as the day grows, spitting, burgeoning, and
flaring out
at the seams
like an infrared sunfish gravid with roe.

As preamble,
the Sun incommodes
all right. Cutting too broad a figure in
a diabolical sky,
its lesion face
peels off, melts down, and recreates itself,
metamorphosing
with vaudeville stamina:
Slowest poker-hot tennis ball on record.
Shuttlecock
warping
the celestial loom. Oozing and malodorous
wound.
Radioactive
brimstone- and lava-lamp. Windbag, rapid-
firing buckshot
torpedoes.
Lethal fenful of clarified pus.   Blazing
white parrot
at red alert
Ulcerated dollop of creamery butter. Light-
stutterer
snagged
on the letter D. Welterweight. Suppurating
ointment ball . . .
and on and on
until the last avatar—a single cormorant
with eye-
branding
plumage—calcifies into heaven's decoy.

~~~~~~

from *Jupiter*

II

Hydrogen, out of it the Universe evolved,
every atom and leaf, marine iguana

and apricot-smelling chanterelle. But my, my,
what alchemy: nondescript H_2

into voluptuous consciousness. I only wish
I could return the favor. Ripe in Jupiter's

wad, the chemical building blocks lie low:
slipshod, aimless, on the brink.

But cellular puberty comes late. I mean
sex among the polymers is something

to ballyhoo. Carbon's atomic wildcard
must form one liaison after another, nimble

as a well-heeled paramour; amino acids
flourish, and primeval broth receive its

genetic bouquet garni before life starts
gunning for something creatural: a bacterium,

an oak, a slipper-shaped liver, or that ultimate
hand-me-down, Man, who minds the world

alien and overawed, a sac of unfelt gestures
and ungestured feelings.

Should life rinse Jupiter's paintbox bayou,
I swear I wouldn't pause a millisecond,

cheering now a pack of viral goons, and now
that molecular epidemic called a rose.

from *Venus*

Low-keyed and perpetual,
a whirling sylph
    whose white robe stripes
                around her; taffeta
wimpled like a nun's headcloth;
        a buxom floozy with a pink boa;
            mummy, whose black
sediment desiccates within; wasp-star
        to Mayan Galileos;
                    an outpatient
wrapped in post-operative gauze;
            Cleopatra in high August—
    her flesh curling
                in a heat mirage
light years
        from Alexandria;
    tacky white pulp
spigoted
        through the belly of a larva;
            the perfect courtesan:
obliging, thick-skinned,
                    and pleated with riddles,
Venus quietly mutates
        in her ivory tower.
                Deep within that
                    libidinous albedo
temperatures are hot enough
        to boil lead,
    pressures
        90 times more unyielding
                    than Earth's.

And though layered cloud-decks
                and haze strata
          seem to breathe
                    like a giant bellows,
heaving and sighing
     every 4 days,
the Venerean cocoon
             is no cheery chrysalis
brewing a damselfly
          or coaxing life
                    into a reticent grub,
   but a sniffling atmosphere
40 miles thick
     of sulphuric, hydrochloric,
     and hydrofluoric acids
all sweating
          like a global terrarium,
          cutthroat, tart, and self-absorbed.
No sphagnum moss
          or polypody fern here,
     where blistering vapors
and rosy bile
     hint at the arson
with which the Universe began.

                    * * *

               Unsullied by moons,
     radiant and blowsy,
               aging
     with almost no midriff bulge,
Venus trills
     her apothecary cloud:
a seasonless queen
   rolling each languorous hip
          so slowly
          no magnetic web forms at all,

or a turbulent spangle,
$\qquad$ shimmery and dead.

$\quad$ Either way,
the planet tilts
$\qquad$ the same face
$\qquad$ Earthward
$\quad$ whenever she's near,
her pearly tonnage
$\qquad$ swinging
$\quad$ like a giant compass
newly risen to our iron heart.

from *Neptune*

IV

Fifteen billion years ago, when the Universe
let rip and, in disciplined panic,
Creation
spewed
mazy star-treacle and resin,
shrinking balls of debut fire smoldered
and
$\qquad$ glitched.
Revolving tantrums tore themselves in,
kernel-tight, then cooler, began shooting off
their
planets
like a brace of dandelions gone to seed.
Even stars don't live forever; old age makes
$\qquad$ the outer
$\qquad$ region
redden and swell (Betelgeuse's radiant flush
in Orion is as much a death-spurt as the whale's
flower
of blood).

Like the body, a star grows larger as it runs
down. Neptune once flecked a coral sun
                                        (yellow
                                            now
as a scrub-diamond) that will puff beet-red
in five billion years, and suck the planets
back
to
where they began.

It's this business of mortality: rallying to
one trickle after another, like a tuber root-
bound
in
a time of drought. I know it's wrong to care
so for worldly things: lanky poplars swaying
                                            like
                                        keening
women, pond-gasses mulling over soil & weed,
the lime-green torches on the candle pine.
I
should
inquire only what is durable, lingering; be
zested, not by things that pass, but by what
                                            will
                                            come
to pass. I know I *should*. But I do not think
I could.

v

You were not summer
            raising the grape.

It may be that in your voice
            I heard crocuses heaving
                        up upon their roots.

but you were mortal as a June bug:
you crapped and wooed,
     were fallible, had allergies.

I knew you were not April
       spurning the ice-hipped weed.

It may be through your eyes
    I saw snapdragons butter-flock
      like popcorn,
but I knew you were not life's
    vesper in the cell.

It may be when you were gone
    it seemed the gypsy moth unshrouded,
      wisteria threned,

but you were mortal as a whistle
down the wind,
    a spark bouquet.

I knew you were not stasis
       bedded in the marl.

And though you were not fall
    silkening the corn,

how I loved you
      in the open heartlands
      of New York.

MARS

The quickest route
from *Candor* to *Chaos*
follows *Coprates*
(the much-traveled
Shit River), through
da Vinci and *Galileo,*
bypassing Bliss,
many moons from *Tranquility.*
But, Romantics, take heart:
you can breakfast
in *Syria,* lunch in *Sinai,*
track the Nile
to its source *(Nilokeras)*
before dinner, and there,
making ablutions to *Osiris,*
win a boon to *Eden,*
where all four rivers
of *Paradise* converge,
then spend the night
in *Pandora,* or with *Ulysses,*
Proteus, or even *Noah,*
in the Land of Gold *(Chryse)*
or by the Leek-green Sea.

That madman Schiaparelli
took one peek
at the Martian tabula rasa
and, daft with the sheer
profusion of matter,
went dub-wild,
leaving here a *Daedalus,*
and there a *Ganges.*
Now we can ankle off
to *Ultima Thule,*

hold the first annual
space games
on the Snows of Olympus,
found a divorce mill
near *Lethes* (Forgetfulness),
and send anal-retentives
to *Coprates.*
I, for one, prefer
my psychodrama straight,
would pass over the equator
at *Cyclops,* ford
the Crossroads of *Charon,*
and follow the river *Styx*
to the Lake of *Hecate,*
the underworld queen.
Or elope to *da Vinci.*

Leonardo, you were the best
inventor: a colossus straddling
the old and the new,
buoyant and uplifting
as the vulture you saw
swoop down at your cradle,
air-strumming with a fringed wing.
Though your predilection
ruled women out, could you deny me
in *Uchronia's* unhurried oasis,
or in *Eos,* that perpetual
rose-toed dawn? And what pigments
you would have made
from these Martian ochers!
Basalt, pumice, limonite,
obsidian . . . I've powdered them all
and mixed them in media,
drawn off umbers
that would make you blink.

You could lose a sorrel gelding
in them, or a roan.

As for Mercury and Venus,
with all their ignominious craters,
whatever will we call *them?*
I get twitchy not knowing.
I'm not asking the Universe
for a stay of execution,
or even that the Logos
declare itself, only
for a quirk or two
my curiosity snags on.
Right now, as I sit here
at the kitchen table,
I want someone to sashay up
to the door, and calmly say,
"Lilith, Ojibway, Rasputin."
I won't plague him
about quarks, cancer, UFO's.
I promise not to ask
about the spurred flagellum.
Only send word. You can trust me.
I listen for a knock, hear none.

Orange-ocher tonight,
ice-age Mars gutters
like a Turner sun.
Brilliant white polar caps
wax and wane with
the weathery (not the growing)
seasons. I know
the rough, bouldery terrain
and volcanic sputum
by heart:
think of the pumice soap,

the obsidian jewelry
(like folds of black satin),
limonite speckled brown
and mustard (on each grain
a fleck of iron:
its own tiny anchor),
the pocked lava rocks
that look like red sponges,
the charred basalt
grilled in mid-pour.

Perhaps Mars
fell together once
long ago, and now,
in an ice age,
its former atmosphere
tucked discreetly
under a polar cap,
awaits the coming
of another spring.
Meanwhile the winds
chafe like emery boards,
carving rock into freeforms
and sway-backed arches.

There was a climate here
once, running water
and the blossom urge,
where sinuous dry riverbeds
stand out now
like veins on a temple.

Yet Olympus Mons,
the largest volcano
in the whole solar system,
may erupt tonight . . .

or not for a century.
I hope it will tonight.
I try to imagine
a mountain 20 miles high:
7 Alps perched
one upon the other's shoulders.

How can it be
this lily-livered flesh
houses the same atoms
that built the Andes
and Himalayas?
I am ashamed
for my lymph nodes:
paltry nubs, even
on the planetary scale.
My arms cascade,
knowing not where to go.
Each day, my mind pitches
its tent elsewhere.
And suddenly,
I have so many toes.

I think how land
forms: massive, bulky,
into stolid plateaus
and great brawny sierras,
and am startled
what touch-and-go
creatures we are
on this minor planet
of a humdrum star.

Wherever I look there's catastrophe:
            craters within craters, volcanic ridges,
                        giant impact basins

like old bull walruses
       gutted by plummeting debris,
              collapsed lava tubes and braided channels,
sand-dune fields 300 feet tall,
       the rift valley in Coprates
              nearly longer than all Africa.

The wind rips by at half the speed of sound,
              then turns tail
                     crossing the equator,
here and there
       scours an oval away
              to show basalt gleaming like mealybugs.

In the Hellas basin
       (I prefer to call Hell's Kitchen),
                     a dust cauldron boils over
to storm-wreck the planet.
       Poor Phobos, the battered child of Mars,
              looms overhead, gouged out and broken.

All around me:
       planet, moon, sun, riverbed, marsh:
                     grew out of cataclysms galore;
nothing ever sprang whole, stays put.
              I feel the earth beneath my feet
                     suddenly shale away;
everywhere I look there's a new disaster,
              and what splintered the mountains
                     made gape the pine.

A spelunker's dream,
       Phobos and Deimos (Fear & Terror)
              chug past, catacombed to the hilt

from all those years
of knocking about, and blacker
than the blackest pitchblende.

They look two prehistoric skulls
unearthed by a Leakey
in some intimate recess of Olduvai Gorge;
you can just make out
the eye socket and jaw, the sunken cheek
and forehead spur.

From another view,
two porous kidneys hover,
long-suffering in the cellar-dark,
as if awaiting a transplant,
begun long ago, that will take yet
another eon to complete.

Till then, I challenge all comers
to the first game of Phoball (Earth rules).
No fear, you'll know my team on sight:
we'll be the ones vaulting skyward
like slow-motion gazelles, thinking how
more than our hearts leap up.

So this is where Elysium lies,
just north of Atlantis,
on the far side of Barsoom:
a velvet landfall, where volcanos
dome gently like saucers
overturned, crater-crowns blend,
no sharp conelike rises ever snag
or grow thorny, and canyons
meander like loose twine. And there,

delirious in our padded cell,
while two moons climb and reclimb
a purple sky, we'll see late-
afternoon clouds lurch overhead,
and the grinding-wheel wind buff
obsidian till it gems in the light.

And, when in summer the bald noon sun
dims behind a dust arroyo, let's
board a nightfreight to Lemuria
(string of opera-length craters)
and, like Laplanders, dot the polar
steppes, while electronic cows nibble
the hoarfrost, their udders ripe with water,
in a land where even ice sublimes.

Love, fly with me to Utopia:
three majestic snow-cowled volcanos
poking up through the sockeye dust.
Like Sherpas, astraddle our mechanical
goats, we'll guide parties
all across the chapped terrain,
early seacliffs and ocher pastures,
tending our rock-leeches that suck
mineral and water till, gorged,
they thud like geckos to the ground.

Come away to the highlands
of Tharsis, and watch the red world
simmer below, teeming with dust-devils
and stiff black shadows,
towering sand-dunes, lava plugs.
Once in a blue sun, when volcanos
heave up grit regular as pearls,
and light runs riot, we'll watch
the sun go darker than the sky,

violet dust-tufts wheel on the horizon,
amber cloudbanks pile, and the whole
of color-crazed Mars ignite.
Come make a dun mare of a wind-carved
arch and, as the rusty sand blows past,
we'll dream ourselves a-gallop
this side of Tranquility, just beyond
Utopia, and through the Martian moors.

SATURN

My sugar daddy bribes me
with a yellow-white brooch
(striped-enamel, diamond,
and ten glittery baguettes)
dangling in a black velvet box.
I stretch up for the honey-pale token, to pin it
on my blouse, over a heart lit like a jack-o'-lantern.
But Saturn lumbers off
with its curio cloudbank,
sky-tethers the icy shoal
elsewhere, padding round
an orbit, just out of reach.

An elliptical blur creeps
into my field of vision, bellowing
light, as I wind the scope down
to such razory focus that Saturn
lies stunned in a hall of mirrors,
hog-tied by the cross hairs, a little green at the pole.
Today lawnmowers studdered, Pekingese yapped, trucks grumbled
through downshift arpeggios; but tonight,
risen in the botherless black,
Saturn's ball of lemon ice
looks so cool and reviving,
I track it like the Golden Fleece.

Millions of vest-pocket moons
hang together as rings
that loop round the planet
like a highway skirting the golden city.
Dusky bright, and god-awful sheer,
they dog the equator, never more than two miles thick:

a sprawling coral reef of tailless comets,
grinding one another
finer and finer, lolloping boulder
to dusty mote as, eddying
down through the crepiest ring,
they pour into a gassy draw.

A tiny moon's constant nagging
shoos the odd guest
from Cassini's division,
an open airway between the rings.
Phobos-sized snowballs tidy it up:
sentinel, roughshod, and devout as gestapos. Wide open,
the rings hustle tons of light (more even
than the planetmain), coming on
so strong in the winter sky
that Dione and Tethys
pale away, like streetwise cats
ambling into the night.

In a seaquarium big enough
Saturn would float! lighter
than rock, or water. I marvel
it even holds together:
hydrogen-clotted ice, frozen
methane and ammonia, all lathered to a gaudy slush,
like Jupiter a bit, only colder, which may be why
the weatherworks and the lazy
cloud-roll idle as they do,
and ammonia freezes out
as a yellow blizzard, snowing
deep into the planetball.

Saturn nods, an outsize natural
sponge, adrift in the galactic shallows;

but far beneath the haze, in a rocky core,
20 Earths could be bedded: stowaway
planets tucked neatly inside,
like sharks napping in an underwater cave. I see the heart
of an artichoke, I remember Goya's *Saturn Devouring a Son.*
We couldn't live here, I'm afraid,
will have to stud the moons
with our kiosks and rotundas, eyeing
from below that striped hammock
bellied across thin air.

A yearlong carnival, known as
Saturnalia, begins with ritual
carving of the rings, when mythic
figures hewn from snowballs—
thousands of Minotaurs, Gorgons,
and Dilemmas, Atlases and Leviathans—all swirl round
the Lord of Halcyon Days, making breezy sacrifice.
For, like Japanese sand-drawings
in an earlier epoch, moon-
carvings are meant to erode, be
dislimbed by the hobnob and bump
of the rings, till not a rack remains.

Saturnalia's a sport time, too,
when Jovian moon-surfers take to Saturn
(another leg of their endless cavort),
flying wildly round the rings' undulating
carpet, or croquet-thwacking debris
in Cassini's division (in danger of being thwacked themselves,
and hauled away by a moonlet-tugboat). You'll see the usual
hawkers and parades, craftspeople, con-men,
homely souvenirs; but only early season,
before the crowds descend, can you watch

the ice-masons hard at work, or hear
the joyous *hoopla*s of the ring-riders.

Entry, *Fodor's Guide to Saturn:*
"Best camera shots
from Iapetus or Phoebe. . . .
Avoid Titan (too cloudy).
The other sherbety moons,
all smackdab in the ringplane, make Saturn appear
utterly ringless:
an agate bulb, with a tally line
summing mid-planet.
But, viewed from Iapetus,
Saturn swivels like a gyroscope,
its hat rim turned

up and down,
while the planetcore stands still.
Daytime, you see back
and darkside of the rings;
nighttime, the sunlit maw.
Only be sure to book a yurt on Planetview (the side facing
Saturn); on the other, glued always to deep space,
you could live out
a lifetime, never knowing
behind you lay
a lighthearted planet,
maizey in a halo of ice."

On Titan, warmed by a hydrogen blanket,
ice-ribbed volcanos jet ammonia
dredged out of a glacial heart. Liquid
and frozen assets uphold an empire
bigger than Mercury, and even a little
like primitive Earth: asphalt plains and hot mineral ponds.

how I'd like to take the waters of Titan, under that
fume-ridden sky,
> where the land's blurred by cherry mist
> and high above, like floating wombs,
> clouds
> tower and swarm, raining down primeval
> bisque, while life waits in the wings.

> Often I dwell on the Big Bang,
> find my heart levied high, and the vision electric,
> am wowed by that arch creativity.
> When I tell people, they flinch
> with terror, want no part of the Ur-inferno,
will not truck with apocalypse. But Paul at the scope, one finger
on the clockdrive, tunes in the Universe
> with the affectionate curiosity of a naturalist.
> And I know, if I trigger the mental
> clockdrive, his mind will gingerly
> backtrack and zoom, run rings round
> the spectral notion of Saturn.

> I say, *"After the never-ending*
> *gas cloud coalesced, the Universe*
> *was all in one place,*
> *and solid: a hard, local object*
> *in an endless ether.''* He smiles,
says, "Wonderful plot!" *"In the beginning was the Word,*
and the Word was a tough, silky ball of hydrogen.''
> He splits the double star, Albireo,
> then pulls back a moment,
> says, "Just imagine the commotion
> of the Big Bang!" We huddle
> in the breathtaking dark, and imagine.

Tonight, what with the moon
keeping so low a profile, the stars
are bright as campfires. Waltzed
around by how many planets? Drenched
in how many groundswells of life?
My saturnine ringleader, pallid-footed, strolls along
with ten swanky moons in tow. And though I'm smitten now
with this giant manticore,
heartwise I know it's only
a panaching fancy: somewhere else
in the odds-on of space, evolution
may be minting a pipefish.

PLUTO

In my 26th year
I left the planet that bore me.
When the Sun had risen
like a golden fish
leaping high into the briny blue,
I put Earth behind me
and traveled light,
sailing out of my flesh
on the first good wind
and barreling tide, to pace out
my tether in the hub of the Sun.
Those whom the darts
of wonder never fret
may think it odd
that on a vapory midday in July
a young woman
might take to the stars.
To these poorer souls,
how can I explain
what their own hearts refuse?
My need to know yammers
like a wild thing in its den.
I see above me Andromeda,
in whose black bosom
galaxies swirl like pastry,
and I am so hungry.

At night I lie awake
in the ruthless Unspoken,
knowing that planets
come to life, bloom,
and die away,
like day lilies opening
one after another

in every nook and cranny
of the Universe,
but I will never see them,
never hear the grumbling
swoon of organ pipes
turning the Martian high winds
into music, never ford
a single interplanetary sea,
never visit the curdling suns
of Orion, even if I plead
with all the fever of a cypress
tilting its spindle limbs
to con summer, piecemeal,
out of early May.

Once, for a year,
I was of nine minds.
And if I lacked nerve
somehow, clinging
to every image as if,
sandbags thrown over
and its balloon out lightweeks
on a flimsy thread,
my life itself might float away,
I knew the trail blazed out
was the way home, too.
How often my teeterboard hips
were desperate to balance
like a schooner's clock.
If I left with the fear of Antaeus,
it was not without
the faith of Eratosthenes,
who dreamt the world round
in a square age.

But now, nine worlds later,
I hug the coastline
of yet another frontier: Pluto,
a planet conjured into being
by the raucous math
of Percival Lowell,
a land bristling with ice,
gray and barren,
where the Sun, nearly doused,
rallies but a paltry sliver
of light, and messages take
ten to twelve hours to field
(imagine the cool, deliberate
chess games, the anxious lovers,
the crises exploding
between communiqués).
A planet-sized enigma
jogging in place, Pluto's moved
little since its discovery,
touring the Sun once
every 248 years.
You could be born in winter,
and never live to spring.

We think of Pluto as an endstop,
or skidding out
like the last skater on a whip,
a land glacial, remote, calm
and phlegmatic.
But right now, while you read
these lines (I swear),
due to an odd perturbation
in their orbits, Neptune and Pluto
are swapping places

in a celestial pas de deux
where the only aerials
are quantum leaps.

If Pluto has a menagerie
of moons, we don't see them
(nor, for that matter, the damned
wallowing in their slime,
or Cocytus, the frozen river of Hades).
No, the Underworld God
keeps his dread secret a moment longer.
About Pluto, we've only
the odd hunch and inkling:
theories pale
as the wings of a linnet.

When our vagabond skiffs
breech the outplanets, I wonder
will we have the presence of mind
to call Pluto's main city *Dis*
(the hellish capital
Dante spoke of), or name
the ferryboat shuttle *Charon,*
the deadspace it cleaves the *Styx.*
Perhaps not.
An ocean is an ocean
after all, whether it loom
from Triton to Pluto
or Southampton to Plymouth.

Where are the Balboas
and the Amerigo Vespuccis
of tomorrow,
hot on the heels of the future,
who will give their names
freely, as if to wives,

as they voyage the spaceblack
waters, always going on
with restless ongoing,
to the end perplexed
by the force that sped them,
and leaving only their names behind?

If Pluto anchors
beyond our sweep, docking
far out along the midnight wharf,
we'll braise
our frontier towns on Triton.
How eerie its floe-broken lands
will seem, with no pink and green
wispy trees of summer
or every so often a blinding white birch.
Could I face only the galaxies
coiled like cobras?

Surely frontier towns
there will always be,
even if "town" seems
too fixed, too stolid,
for anything so mercurial
as "frontier" to be caught with.
Deep in the mountainsides,
where the temperature
is least likely to skitter,
we'll build
our snuggeries and hives,
be cave dwellers again.
It's as if, flummoxed
by the shock of living,
we step by step restage it,
driven to the most far-reaching
ritual. Like a catechism,

we begin again: the cave dweller,
the trapper, the trader,
the explorer; the self-reliance,
the hope, the patience,
the invention: wrapped in our past
as we breathe down
the glistening neck of the future.

Forgive my brain
its wanton poaching
on an earlier estate,
but such frontier talk
leads me back to da Vinci.

Leonardo, come steal
into the chamber of my thought
again. How I miss
that nomadic mind of yours,
always at red-alert
and surging like a furnace.
Often I dream that,
like a horse flinching
to keelhaul a fly,
I might shed the centuries
and give you a motor
or a fixed wing.
Had you erred into my bed
and body last night,
I could not hold you dearer.

What sort of woman can it be
who feels at home
in all the Universe,
and yet nowhere on Earth,
who loves equally
what's living and ash?

I can't seem to overlook
the context
in which I live,
this collection of processes
I call my life,
even though the flower
be indifferent to my pleasure,
and the honeybee virus
dragging its genetic pollen
from one cell to another
be blind to my despotic ways.
One sultry morning
I found a sneaker print
in the mud, whose herringbone grid
looked like a trilobite fossil.
How you would marvel
at the alchemy of line.
All day I suffered
that I couldn't tell you.

The bread mold and I
have much in common.
We're both alive.
The wardrobe of our cells
is identical. We speak
the same genetic code.
The death of a star
gave each of us life.
But imagine
a brandspanking new
biology. Just as
when a window
abruptly flies open
the room grows airy
and floods with light,
so awakening to
an alien lifeform

will transfigure
how we think of ourselves
and our lives.
In my bony wrist alone,
the DNA could spin a yarn
filling thousands and thousands
of library volumes.
But one day we'll browse
in the stacks of other galaxies.
Given the sweet generosity of time
that permits the bluegreen algae
and the polar bear,
the cosmic flannel
must be puckered with life.
My bad habits charm me now
with reckless appeal;
we may be the habit of the Universe.

Today in the locker room,
under the dryer,
threshing my long hair
in a wind that might have swept
off the Gobi or Kalahari,
I let my thought freefall
from Hercules, into whose arms
our Sun is rushing,
to the sky thick with planets
and ghostly neutrinos,
how through a telescope
color-flocked nebulae
look like cameos:
black-and-white miniatures
of themselves.

While such visions
and ripe polychotomies
waylaid me,

fleshed-up women
paraded by, whose breasts
swung like pendulums
chiming their hours,
and tummy-rises blurred
to an iridescent ripple.
Somewhere
far down the locker row
a woman's voice,
like an eagle or kite,
balanced on a rising column of air.
I stepped out onto the beach
of our galaxy
and, as my hair became a trellis
in the solar wind, I wedded
that shining carapace of the future.

Once, for a year, my thoughts
gathered like clouds
into skycoves and jetties.
Entombed in a so-so body
coloring, I was perfectly wowed
by the Joseph-coat planets,
the lurid gas ribbons
and sherbety pastels,
Jupiter's organic chowder,
the saturnine rings bleeding light.

I consulted the moon
like a crystal ball.
I boned up on the flinty
inner planets, whose craters
do-si-do for miles.
I steered by Sirius,
the effervescent guide.
I pored over our bio-heirlooms

like a medium
needing to feel the murderer's glove.
I winnowed, I delved,
I compassed, I schooled,
breezing from one delicate
science to the next
with the high-flying rapture
of a bird of prey.
My heart jingled,
full of its loose change.

I return to Earth now
as if to a previous thought,
alien and out of place,
like a woman who,
waking too early each day,
finds it dark yet
and all the world asleep.
But how could my clamorous heart
lie abed, knowing all of Creation
has been up for hours?

Wife of Light

(1978)

MOTHER

Mama's just blown in from Egypt,
full of mummy-lore, mishap,
river life, and beggars;
toting quietly hued soapstone
scarabs, then fabric, jewels,
and bazaar-haggled goods;
pausing half a breath
to praise the guide
(savvy with hieroglyphics),
or damn the cuisine,
wince at the hygiene,
or, burbling spicy as the Nile,
hymn the feluccas at sunset,
whose huge linen sails,
bloating like ghosts,
patrol the slim swift river.

Round her neck she wears
a gold cartouche of her name:
hieroglyphs:
"cricket, bird, doorlatch, mouth, bird."
And yes, she *is* clicky and pert
as a cricket, twittery as a finch,
wedded to home-things
scrutably as a doorlatch,
gabby and bright, and game to fly off
to any grotto or seaport,
savanna or spa, glacier or oasis,
like a royal bird jaded by a single nest.

With her "Let's get crackin',"
and her "Howdja do,"
and her "Time's a-wastin',"
and her stiff coiffed hair,

and her soft winning smile,
and her livewire touring
from glowworm drippy caves
tilted deep in New Zealand
to Troy, Masada, Moscow or Bali Hai,

she is like a wild grain
waving its tassel
at the broiling summer sun:
an explosion of bud,
untroubled by pondering,
blues, or jet lag.
Churning and singable as the Nile,
she is life, and life
is what she brings.

NEW HOUSE

We bought a house hand-me-down
and complete, packed with all the gear
family life engenders: cameras,
clothing, junk and antiques,
vibrator, bowling ball, pans and glasses.

Every knickknack knows gossip
I have no right to, about a Mr. Norton
who lived, bred, and boozed there.
I'm told he died of gluttony
in middle age, towards the end

bloating like a pufferfish. Now
suddenly I've acquired
someone's life, as if it were a fondue pot
or a hedge cutter. His initial
still rules the hall linoleum.

There are mortgages and taxes
and a pool to skim daily,
poison ivy to uproot, grass to mow,
doors to lock. And me
with no steady job guaranteed.

Soon I'll leave the little garret
I've spent five years in, groomed
and combed and grown used to,
where I bedded my lover
and housed my jubilation, relaxed,

fretted, and pined, grew used to.
A roommate once had an Afghan hound
with brown eyes like quicksand,

and such long spindly legs
it never could lie down right.

I used to watch
the poor beautiful creature
circle, fold and unfold and fold
its legs again, trying,
for all the world, just to settle.

ODE TO AN APPALOOSA STALLION

Spotted veteran of love,
you were made for fucking.
Wooing the mare with a tender nuzzle,
you rub her nether petals
till they open
pink and dewy as a magnolia,
before you climb aboard
and set your hips a-bucking.

I see your white hide crawl,
black rosettes shudder
(like a scoopful of coal
dropping through snow),
and come alive
at the snort of your sunburnt nose,
your sweetbags twitching
peppery as stars.

If only I could have
the blunt fury of your limbs,
yowl and pump
like a desperado,
feel the sun on my neck
burning old as a motto,
then life coming,
the wheat spellbound in the fields.

SONG OF π

What lengths I've gone to
hoiking this gap-toothed
carcass up, as I barrel
out past horizon's bluff,
every digit pacing
like a Tennessee walker,
unable to break even,
come round. Still,
I invent myself daily:
buxom 3's, coathanger 2's,
fetal 9's, 4's blowing
always to the west,
snowman 8's, runnel 1's,
and now and then
a single tantalizing 0
(whose frogspawn
could make one whole).
Thus I evolve, think,
quibble, and revise
on the spot, as though
daft with some perpetual
misgiving: 3.14 . . .
or rather 3.142 . . . I mean
3.1416 . . . no, 3.14159 . . .
ad infinitum . . . :
a concatenation of qualms
limping across the page
to no fixed result:
skittish, mazy,
decimated, unrepeating,
constant but runic,
at loose ends; while new
factors, a hair's breadth
more discrete, merely

winch the total sequence
tighter. Dwindling
ciphers trail behind me
like outmoded deities,
pleading to expire
in some perfect wholeness—
be finite, tally, nothing spare.
And so I hold out for that
wish-ribbed strand, perhaps
just over the next abscissa,
when the last of my last
fraction rounds off, and in one
spine-humming flash I feel
the common denominator
blaze through.

CRITICAL MASS

As I inch into Cayuga's neutral bed,
weeds begin to tick like fingers.

I can hear death hovering in the cell,
in the *cleat, cleat, cleat* of a wind-ripped

hickory, but am loath to unsaddle my mulish
brain of its radiant trappings: the fire-

bellied toads and mahogany horse chestnuts,
vegetarian crawdads digging down

to water level below the outlying cornfield,
the plaintive moan of an opossum's cantata.

And I am green to the tailwinds that gypsy
my thought so: gaping, misfit, and unplumbable.

Even the water spider seems to know
his belongings. I watch the plier legs open

and close, filled with the skittling lope
of him. And I am witless to the dynamo

revving my bustled heart when a siege of quail
fly cover at lake bend. And I am lame

to fathom this napalm wonder I cannot douse
even in the cool of the daybreak.

GEORGE SAND, ADDRESSING HER MIND, AT 50

Brain, old pensioner,
for years of loyal and fretful service,
        what honorarium will do?
            A silver watch
    to tell minute vistas by,
while 60 cogs a minute
        leave you, winded, to your slackening
                haste?
    A pen seeping bile
            from its whale-black innards?

You, who never dressed before noon!
        I find you out
    early: doing sums, mending fences,
knitting yarns. Here,
        let me clink my fork
            against the glass,
    rise to the occasion,
        my shabby matron, my old grass-gypsy,

and swear, though you lie
in comic disarray,
            pilled and pickled in your juices,
    your skirts frayed and gussetted,
        that you once ploughed furrows
straight as statutes,
            once, with your pack of hunting dogs,
    ran deep into far sloughy fields
to snare game,
            once hooted fashion,
        once tupped and raved,
once cheered, fueled, dabbled, quaffed,

tracked down, bled, bouqueted, and wallowed
in ideas,
covering their waterfront
like a sailor's whore, who,
sleeping with all, belonged to none.

QUIXOTE

What plagues the store-bought world is tedium.
Hash most nights. Beef shanks-and-sockets.
Lentils! On Sunday, boiled bones and *Te Deum.*
Buttoning and unbuttoning each other's pockets.

This night more sequined than a jaguar's hide
the moon is luminous, a white fleshy scar.
Time is a kneeling animal. People chide
me for being short of sense, but *they* are
short of wonder. Inbred. Inert. In cahoots. In lieu.
They spend their lives like dull brass coins,
while I crack open a world or two:
life's torpor is the blazing savanna of my loins.

So let me flail bug-eyed at a windmill's bark,
steal vision's pass key, and rifle the dark.

LIFE SENTENCE

Aside from the eggs like tiny appaloosas
cantering through my body's tide; the sun
always in the sky, and the ululation
of the seasons; aside from the winter/spring
polemic quibbling over a dry seedpod till it
sounds like a hooded mamba or a harpist;
aside from how grackles in a pile of hay
swear blue-jesus to con the moon into
one more spin around the dancing floor
and never notice the lean shafts lifting,
how *they* are lifting, till ploughed land's
widewale nap is lost in a flight of breakneck
clouds; aside from that vague psoriasis
of the spirit that threatens my bone-house
with foreclosure, the brainpantry teeming,
and the will as bloodthirsty as a tick; I mean
aside from all these obvious concessions,
I keep asking myself: what does gravity demand?

MADAME BOVARY TO HER LOVER

Tuesday. The word sounds as far away
        as Florence. The backside of the moon
       is closer than tuesday!
   Tell me the winds, like a bagpipe skirling,
hail from a duchy
              fabulous as tuesday.
    The hot-blooded sun, now flitting
down my neck, now filling my room
     with its gold soliloquy,
  couldn't burn from a place
         more remote than tuesday.

My heart spends what it can least afford,
     a hundred times a day
         climbs aboard a jitney
   bound for tuesday; how shall I bear
its sweet treachery till tuesday?
          I'll work, I'll tidy, I'll garden,
  I'll do. I'll browse through scores
weighty as linen, but tuesday,
    tuesday dear as a pardon,

  tuesday as unlikely as the Serengeti,
       tuesday, when you arch above me
    like a melody,
      when you sail through my limbs
  on a breeze fresh as a colt,
    tuesday will harvest my mood,
my thought, tuesday rustle my whims,
     tuesday grow in my life
       like a weed.

A shadow, oblique, in a dream is tuesday!
Only a China clipper, swayed off course,
a tunic of kelp choking its bow,
might chance on an island
extravagant as tuesday.
Nut-sweet as tuesday. Lush and willowy
and green as tuesday. Come, swear to me
that in your blithe pursuance
of theater, soirées, and ortolans,
you won't know a savory breath
till tuesday!

MYSTIC COMMUNION OF CLOCKS

There being no mystic communion of clocks
    it hardly matters when this autumn breeze
    wheeled down from the sun
    to make leaves skirt pavement like a million lemmings

An event is such a little piece of time-and-space
    you can mail it through the slotted eye of a cat
    we all pretty much agree
    words just fret the bowed neck of time

So it's nothing to say that at 96 below
    on this lovely fall day in arctic Siberia
    a young woman carried home her daily milk
    not in a bottle but under her arm in a slab

Or that precisely at five o'clock in the evening
    the Trans-Siberian express tore streaks of iron
    from the vastness of nothing
    and ran hell-bent to the extremities of nowhere

ANNE DONNE TO HER HUSBAND

Come to bed, Jack, the candle's shed
to its waxy skirt, and I can read
    your straying wits by the moon.
A brain-fly must be buzzing your head!
    What is it now, that new ice, sheeting
the pond like a scald on hot milk? The swoon
    of dam-water, like a silent diphthong?
Lucky pond, to hold your gaze so long.

My eiderdown is greener than a glade;
you gave it me yourself, high
    when you dubbed me your *new found land,*
and swore, my continents your quest, you'd trade
    along the shores of my dark timbered eyes,
where unwooed lusheries of life meander,
    and time drops sail like a ketch in a lagoon.
Well, then, what keeps you?

Come away from the window!
You get ideas like other men catch cold.
    Mid-morning, a trifle waylaid you again,
and now your eyes, like twin hyenas,
    pick dinner in the slivery light
from the moon. Enough of your lyric flight!
    Enough peeking under the night's black shirt!
All day, you've been sickening with a verse.

For God's sake, quit gaming
with love, in poems abstruse, or as physical
    as if you were a physical
man. Maybe this one you'll title "Love's Dynasty,"
    and begin with a sunset, lying

on the horizon like an eel
   twitching its thick brown hide,
then hint at things matrimonial.

   And who'll guess that tonight, upright as an easel,
you've earth on the brain, not me.
   Though I'd tie you in lawless knots
if I could, my heart knows
   no rhetoric but your name,
Jack, that, like a doomed colonial,
   sails out with a seed-chest full of hope,
and raises so little crop.

   How can I compete with a vision?
What holy logic could my wiles defy?
   Your muse that's fat and sassy
as a cow, could I stint her even one
   of her piquancies? Her powwows? Her sprees?
What would it cost, in hard daily coin,
   if I shook you loose from this reverie?
I am not love's barrister (wish I were),

   but an offput woman on a night growing bleaker,
and night was never longer, or woman weaker.

SWEEP ME THROUGH YOUR MANY-CHAMBERED HEART

Sweep me through your many-chambered heart
if you like, or leave me here, flushed
amid the sap-ooze and blossom: one more dish
in the banquet called April, or think me hard-
won all your days full of women. Weeks
later, still I felt your arms around
me like a shackle, heard all the sundown
wizardries the fired body speaks.
Tell me why, if it was no more than this,
the unmuddled tumble, the renegade kiss,
today, rapt in a still life and unaware,
my paintbrush dropped like an amber hawk;
thinking I'd heard your footfall on the stair,
I listened, heartwise, for the knock.

A. R. AMMONS AMID THE FUNGI

You say: segmented worms
roll back their saddles
during copulation.

And I say: yes, and pine bristles
like a boar's back.

And you say: red-capped fungi
will fabric the spring.

And I say: yes, and woodchucks
in hibernation are breathing
only ten times an hour.

And you say: shape & form & saliences.
And I say: verbal pliés, acoustic fatigue,

and do you read lodestars and cereal boxes?
And you say: yes, and navigation manuals,
place mats, and hurricane charts.

And I say: do you mind that it's colder
than a polar bear's menses? or that a cat
in a black hole in space becomes linguini?

I say: did you know that from Rimbaud
you get barium and radium, Bim, Bram,
mab, braid, drum, dram, daub, raid?

And you say: yes, and also bird & Brad,
Baird & Mau & Ra & Maud. And axolotl
is also good, have you tried vineyard yet?

And I say: yes, and that pockmarked
aluminum prop that we call a moon
answers directly to Mission Control.

And you say: yes, that trollop's
on a tether of Tang; she put the rill
in Rilke, you know what I mean?

And I say: yes, a bone knits and
a river purls, and I've always
admired your southern kraal.

And you say: jejune, and knee-deep
in the magma.
And I say: this is not the Hebrew letter
for Jehovah.

And you say: one thing about death—
it's hereditary.

And I say: where the hell are we
and, incidentally, how the hell is it here?
Isn't a friend someone to tread water with?

And you say: the asylum of idle chatter
is wide open.

ENTREATY

Sir, if you love me, hold me to life
            as to a promise,
provide for my ramshackle age.
Never will I be gibbous like the moon,
childfull and eager
            all the tot-centered day.
Though I conjure pelicans
            out of ice-tinged barbwire,
or lathe heaven into a shrinkproof hour,
others know by instinct
            what I never learned:
how to crochet raggedy minutes into spells,
            spells into days.

Sir, if you love me, teach me to collect
            my galloping hopes;
how to jam work's merciful fabric
into each hollow of a routine month;
how to greet life
            blazing like the pillars of Troy
and not char to rubble, not turn sour;
how to trot out and lunge the stabled heart
on riderless calms
            in the deathwatch of winter.

Sir, if you love me, teach me to thrive
without you,
            to be my own genesis.

I'm sick of the night
deep as a lagoon,
its plum waters
crazed with larvae,
and the egret stars
picking, picking,
as their bills
garble moonlight
to fine glitter;

dog-tired of the spring days
thick as hops,
when seedpods lie wet
in their golden hulls,
and the streetlamps at dusk
echo and re-echo
a bluesy sun;

fed up with the *chee chee*
of the cardinals,
and the black quilted
cloud cover over the mountain,
and the hand-brogue
of the deaf-mute
across the road,
yes, and the loudmouthed
yahoo next door;
have had enough now
of the kites
circling, circling
like polishing rags,
and the lake tilting
its wet thighs
around a bend,

and the jet honing
a white arc
from zenith to horizon;

I'm sick to death
of all the Halloweens
and Easters,
and the neighbor girls
loping through the yard:
(each pelvis a-flutter
like a pair of wings)
the mud ripe
in the mid-August heat,
the popsongs,
the gone-sours,
the setbacks, the blights,
the cartwheel heart
where love careens,
all the little dismals
and the giant dreams.

THE ELEMENTS

Her face. She forms it
with the pepper of makeup
on skin gelled clean,
daubs on philters
that haven't changed
since Grecian girls
picked wild tansy
to warm their cheeks
like seaslopes bending
the Mediterranean sun.

She pore-tugs
with astringent ice,
beauty grains, and the pulpy
green meat of an avocado.
Scoured, her face feels
brittle as taffeta, and
ready for its slipstream
of super-luminous gloss.
Color she doles out
like black-currant jam.

What she tells herself
varies from day to day: she's
a victim of habit, washed-out,
or wan, or an *echt* modern woman,
or a Creole artist. And besides,
who can say it's not Quechua
warpaint—tom-tom of rouge
drummed into the bone? Anything
but that grave in the cell.

Each morning she rebegins
her saga of color: bugle-shaped

eyes drawn black as lava
float gaily on phosphorescent lids.
She dips into her bag of notions
for some salve to make her toll
like a bell rung by Abelard,
or cast by El Greco:
Scheherazade of the bathroom,
victim of the molecule.

DRIVING THROUGH FARM COUNTRY AT SUNSET

As I drive through farm country,
a damp reek brewing by the roadway
hits me. Manure, cut grass, honeysuckle,
spearmint. The air feels light as rusk.
And I want to lie down in the newly turned
earth, amid the wheat-chaff and the chicory,
while sunlight creeps up a mountainside

off in the distant whelm of color.
Each cemetery, flanked by poplars, looks ready
to play as a chess set. A dozen washloads
blow on the line, sock lanterns ablaze,
towels bellied like a schooner's rigging.
In a dogwood's petaled salon, bees leave
their pollen footprints as calling cards.

The occasional samba of a dragonfly
tightens the puffy-lidded dusk.
Clouds begin to curdle overhead. And I want
to lie down with you in this boggy dirt,
our legs rubbing like locusts'.
I want you here with the scallions
sweet in the night air, to lie down with you
heavy in my arms, and take root.

I SHOULD HAVE TREKKED WITH SCOTT
TO ANTARCTICA

I should have trekked with Scott to Antarctica
and ditched my ghost there, so I'd be numb
as prairie ice by now, free from love's arsenic
to-ing and fro-ing, my hope fitful as a swannery.

I should have lived heartsimple as a nun,
worn my habits like silk, said buckshot Hail Marys,
been exempt from the fiery greens of summer
and your gaze overflowing my saucer eyes.

I should have been a thermal, or the windage
in a breeze left by the swift absence of a nighthawk,
been immune to all the heady fret and vigil
when doubt sails cockeyed as an ice yacht.

Or I should have been a gypsy fit to besot you,
rivet you with spells, puzzle and haunt you,
ripe as a pomegranate, a sensual stampede,
not this plain young woman with an abstract need.

PERIOD PIECE

Moon, whose name I bear, whose likeness
like a coin I wear on my thigh,

Moon bleeding light across the sky,
tally me a bonus month on your ledger,

before this light and tender anger swells.
You who fan the fever in my cells,

who take a fine fettle and curdle it brainsick,
or turn a heart bright as nettle rash

choleric, Moon be ghostly, run your rings
round me with sweet dereliction,

drain the red lava from my womb
if you must. Grip my bowels with cramps

thick as a simoom, but spare me
the trumpeting frets and the jealousies,

the love-yowls, the warps of reason,
the willies, the riptides, the alarms,

the old woes I exhume like unquiet corpses,
the boohoos, and the dread,

the nuggets of self-pity glowing
like ore in a swamp-black season.

Moon, white as garlic
in the cauldron of my misery,

today your silent weather in the vein
swept through my bone house

like a cyclone, cut the delicate seines
my trawlers fix in wonder's lush terrain,

bowled a shock wave so razing
my bubbly spirits decanted to still-wine.

Cares that daily fade or lie low
hogged front-row-center in the bleachers

of my despair and there, solemn
as Kewpie dolls, began to heckle and hoot.

My lover I tried to box into absolutes,
pelting him with a cairn of chaos.

I hung round his neck like an albatross.
I told him my heart was black as a nimbus,

squirrely, young, and disloyal as dross,
then watched his eyes grow heavy as ingots.

Moon, I am like a carpet you flog.
I, who am too far from the cave

for worship, too far from the grave
to nod and cry quits, where do I send my protest,

my plea? Whom do I lobby for redress,
what throat do I slit on what altar?

Moon, in whose lumbering wake
my blood swarms, humor me: stand still

in the heavens, deliver me from all this
dolor and fugue (I'd sooner

you looted my soul than my mood),
spare me your rod and your cane.

Pale goblin I waltz with each night,
if you fancy me so, feed your ivory yen

and drink my fluids all, espouse me,
wed me to oblivion. For I am like a heron

on your South China junk. Slip off
the gold wafery collar that keeps

mortality but a swallow away,
and you can clasp me forever

to your wide white chest,
make me your concubine, your dalliance.

Snatch me now in the dead of night.
Only, Moon, be merciful to your wife of light.

WHERE PAUL WAS BORN

On a fog-cowled island
bobbing in the North Sea
like an iceberg—
little more than a chip
on Europe's shoulder;
next to the butcher shop
and across from the dry-goods
in a one-horse, twenty-pub,
cod-ridden town smackdab
in the Midlands, and called
Eckington;
hemmed in by coal mines
and the Sitwell acreage
where he first saw holly
growing wild: unplaited
and prickly all summer's
dead heat; in a row house
that sprawled up, not along
(flatiron warming
on the coals, chenille tablecloth
laid with empty jam jars
and mixed crockery, the gaslight
begging for another penny);
three flights high
in an attic room overlooking
the Roman church and well spots
(from there to eye's limit,
khaki & green fields
sprouting wheat and cabbage);
in the blue bedroom,
under the eiderdown,
on a mattress fretted
with switchbacks and gullies;
out of a Saxon woman

with gray eyes, who was born
on Market Street,
married there, and, lifelong,
moved only ten yards or so;
through her tipped gullet:
queer, but sounder than my own;
knee-deep in her spine;
from a womb they unlatched
and tilted down like a chute;
covered with umbilical sackcloth
from the start, Paul landed
in this world on his feet.

ADDENDUM

And isn't it enough that the mind's caliper
widens to take in a log, can also

accommodate the hollow bones of a blackbird
flying elliptically to pinion a field,

does not overlook the sun bleaching the sky,
or how pinecone trees effloresce

into a highrise of spiny sea urchins and then
handgrenades frozen at the moment of explosion,

and never misses the dark hot muscle of a tuna;

I've got lots of sensibility and no common sense;
isn't it better to lie low while the universe bombards,

to ride out the pendulation of the seasons,
straining not so often to embrace the moon, but more

to render it embraceable; isn't it enough
that one branch, rocking before a storm, can gather

the lines of twilight like threads in cool fresh sheets;
and isn't it enough that all creeks flow seaward;

isn't it enough that riverbanks come in pairs?

CURTAINS OF GOLDENROD

Where curtains of goldenrod, dry
after their season's stiff yellow plume,
made hilltop a chamber, and a dozen blues
like confluent rivers of sky, met,
there, beneath the wild hay, you took me,
on a horseblanket, in a polar month,
sun hot on our heels, as well as our brains,
turning me nimbly on forehand and haunch,
while jets passed over like breaking waves.
I have scratches where the straw weeds chafed;
you made me willow like the bending grain.
Above, your eyes looked bluer than two ermine
in winter, bluer than the day's high nape.
Even the sky seemed to begin with your face.

OF COURSE THE EARTH WON'T STOP

Of course the Earth won't stop
if you never uprush my steps again,
all winning talk and agile limbs.
The whiskery mountains,
in whose five o'clock shadow we loved, won't up
and fly apart. Geese will mob again,
blackening the sky like a shake of pepper,
coffee beans still look like tiny twats, paupers
sign their names with a flourish,
cattle moan like banshees to be fed, the Earth
go on its green, evitable way,
full of come-hither meadowgrass
waving and waving
and waving, under a moon round as an abbess.

Only life's eager whittler will hollow
me out by seconds, chip bark
off living wood, my heart
lie thwarted as a wing-clipped swallow
each time I confuse its muffled beating
for your heel-skip on the landing.
I'll remember how we loved: hot
and smoking as the Caribbean sun,
and the blues will settle in my ribcart
like a fog, my spirit blight, my shanties rot.
Days
will drag their long carcasses on
forever, dull as ditchwater, blank arrays.
Then loss will jimmy my bones apart,
till I die from the draft in my heart.

Scanning the beach:
a sail distends its bubble throat
like a lizard in heat, stray cats
go slow-gait through palms and mimosas
toying with the carcass of a beetle,
sandfleas tick away at my heels
like kamikaze pilots.

           In the kitchen
Millicent scales red snapper; the silk fish
we'll eat on the veranda.

I can account for hydra-headed coral,
atomic weights, salmonella poison,
beetles surviving unchanged for centuries,
lemur feet flat as tiny pancakes,
even life in a pocket of RNA.

But as for how all flesh arose
from that slimy web of muck and weed,
how eyes, brains, nerves sprang
from the interface of plankton and mammal,

all I hear is the thunder of water
on a tin sieve. Crash and caterwaul
as waves crack bone off the coral reef:
an orchestrated bribe, perhaps,
nothing less than lunacy.

ODE TO THE ALIEN

Beast, I've known you
in all love's countries, in a baby's face
   knotted like walnut meat,
         in the crippled obbligato
   of a polio-stricken friend,
in my father's eyes
   pouchy as two marsupials,
         in the grizzly radiance
of a winter sunset, in my lover's arm
   veined like the Blue Ridge Mountains.
To me, you are beautiful
         until proven ugly.

Anyway, I'm no cosmic royalty
either: I'm a bastard of matter
   descended from countless rapes
         and invasions
   of cell upon cell upon cell.
I crawled out of slime;
   I swung through the jungles
         of Madagascar;
I drew wildebeest on the caves at Lascaux;
         I lived a grim life
   hunting peccary and maize
in some godforsaken mudhole in the veldt.

I may squeal
   from the pointy terror of a wasp,
or shun the breezy rhetoric
         of a fire;
but, whatever your form, gait, or healing,
   you are no beast to me,

I who am less than a heart-flutter
     from the brute,
          I who have been beastly so long.
Like me, you are that pool
          of quicksilver in the mist,
     fluid, shimmery, fleeing, called life.

          And life, full of pratfall and poise,
     life where a bit of frost
one morning can turn barbed wire
          into a string of stars,
     life aromatic with red-hot pizazz
drumming ha-cha-cha
          through every blurt, nub, sag,
          pang, twitch, war, bloom of it,
life as unlikely as a pelican, or a thunderclap,
     life's our tour of duty
          on our far-flung planets,
          our cage, our dole, our reverie.

     Have you arts?
     Do waves dash over your brain
          like tide along a rocky coast?
Does your moon slide
     into the night's back pocket,
          just full when it begins to wane,
so that all joy seems interim?
          Are you flummoxed by that millpond,
deep within the atom, rippling out to every star?
          Even if your blood is quarried,
I pray you well,
     and hope my prayer your tonic.

          I sit at my desk now
          like a tiny proprietor,

a cottage industry in every cell.
   Diversity is my middle name.
My blood runs laps;
         I doubt yours does,
            but we share an abstract fever
               called thought,
a common swelter of a sun.
So, Beast, pause a moment,
            you are welcome here.
      I am life, and life loves life.

A FINE, A PRIVATE PLACE

He took her one day
under the blue horizon
where long sea fingers
parted like beads
hitched in the doorway
of an opium den,
and canyons mazed the deep
reef with hollows,
cul-de-sacs, and narrow boudoirs,
and had to ask twice
before she understood
his stroking her arm
with a marine feather
slobbery as aloe pulp
was wooing, or saw the octopus
in his swimsuit
stretch one tentacle
and ripple its silky bag.

While bubbles rose
like globs of mercury,
they made love
mask to mask, floating
with oceans of air between them,
she his sea-geisha
in an orange kimono
of belts and vests,
her lacquered hair waving,
as indigo hamlets
tattooed the vista,
and sunlight
cut through the water,
twisting its knives
into corridors of light.

His sandy hair
and sea-blue eyes,
his kelp-thin waist
and chest ribbed wider
than a sandbar
where muscles domed
clear and taut as shells
(freckled cowries,
flat, brawny scallops
the color of dawn),
his sea-battered hands
gripping her thighs
like tawny starfish
and drawing her close
as a pirate vessel
to let her board:
who was this she loved?

Overhead, sponges
sweating raw color
jutted from a coral arch,
clown wrasses
hovered like fireworks,
and somewhere an abalone opened
its silver wings.
Part of a lusty dream
under aspic, her hips rolled
like a Spanish galleon,
her eyes swam
and chest began to heave.
Gasps melted on the tide.
Knowing she would soon be
breathless as her tank,
he pumped his brine
deep within her,
letting sea water drive it

through petals
delicate as anemone veils
to the dark purpose
of a conch-shaped womb.
An ear to her loins
would have heard the sea roar.

When panting ebbed,
and he signaled *Okay?*
as lovers have asked,
land or waterbound
since time heaved ho,
he led her to safety:
shallower realms,
heading back toward
the boat's even keel,
though ocean still petted her
cell by cell, murmuring
along her legs and neck,
caressing her
with pale, endless arms.

Later, she thought often
of that blue boudoir,
pillow-soft and filled
with cascading light,
where together
they'd made a bell
that dumbly clanged
beneath the waves
and minutes lurched
like mountain goats.
She could still see
the quilted mosaics
that were fish
twitching spangles overhead,

still feel the ocean
inside and out, turning her
evolution around.

She thought of it miles
and fathoms away, often,
at odd moments: watching
the minnow snowflakes
dip against the windowframe,
holding a sponge
idly under tap-gush,
sinking her teeth
into the cleft
of a voluptuous peach.

AMPHIBIANS

All season we've tried
        to keep frogs from diving
    deeper into the chlorine-laced pool.
We run, skimmers twitching,
        to scoop them out; but no use.
    Three frogs dead in the filter
again today. Weightless things,
        water-pithed,
    their limbs cast open
(wider than in fieldlife),
            each muscle lax
        as a broken shade. Wan eyes
hug shut, as if in light contemplation.
        And out of sight,
    beneath the limp, leathery skin,
a genetic code mixes
            like alphabet soup,
        each tiny ladder split rungless now
for this final climb down to earth.

WHALE SONGS

Speaking in storm language,
a humpback, before it blows,
lows a mournful ballad
in the salad-krill sea, murmurs
deep dirges; like a demiurge,
it booms from Erb to Santa Cruz,
bog low, its foghorn a thick liqueur.

Crepe black as a funeral procession,
the pod glides, mummer-deft,
through galloping brine,
each whale singing the same
runaway, roundelay tune:

Dry fingers rub, drag, drub
a taut balloon. Glottal stops. Pops.
Dry fingers resume, then, ringing
skeletal chimes, they ping
and rhyme—villanelles, canticles,
even a Gregorian done on ton tongues

as, trapped below the consciousness
of air, hungry, or wooing,
or lamenting slaughter,
jazzy or appalled,
they beat against the wailing wall
of water, voices all
in the marzipany murk they swim,
invisible but for their songs.

And often they raise high
as angels' eyes a refrain
swoony as the sea, question-mad
sad, all interrogatives, as if

trying to fathom the fathomless
reach from ladle-shaped ocean,
scurrilous surf, to breach-birth
upon beach and blue algae's cradle.

Sleek black troubadours
playing their own pipes, each body
a mouth organ, each shape a daguerreotype
of an oblate friar caroling,
they migrate, glad to chain rattle
and banshee moan, roaming the seas
like uneasy spirits, a song on their bones.

NIGHT FLIGHT

I

At 12,000 feet, lights below
dot the blackness as if by rule,
fill our ever-arranging eyes
with sparkling motifs, a parole of order
vast, doping, and certain.

But suppose those gold temple bells
chime only in the mind.
Suppose that sheen is not geometry,
but mere angling, a peasant code
for the manorless void.

Then the apparent samba of geranium buds
banking to the light
would be an accident of faith
at a winter window.

Then ice honeycombed by chickenwire,
at daybreak, would be certain knowledge.
Then finding hieroglyphics
of sparrow tracks in the snow
would be cause to send telegrams
and unfurl all our flags.

Then the banana republic of the heart
would be everything.

II

In the measured world below
lie unmapped constellations:
a winged camel, a milkman, a bee-clustered hive.

We will never name them
any more than the lit veils
on the skyline, or the gold membranes
as city lights float under us
the tracery of a fluorescent sea creature
on a moonless reef,
its backbone a tilted highway
glittering to the horizon,
neon hubs its organs and, in between,
the webbed tinsel of suburbia.

III

Red lights in the cockpit.
A pilot cradles the wheel's two uplifted arms,
as unerring numbers
count backward to zero.
Their message is not new.
Drifting mindful somewhere
between the cities and the moon,
he watches numbers flicker,
as if to unravel them
and name their starry sum,
as if he could speak
the patois of sheer light.

CLIMBING OUT

For Martin

Blue fluid in my limbs,
momentum buoys me up
at take-off speed
as I lose ground for that puzzle
older than hearsay,
whose thralldom is a witless bird
navigating a meadow.

Then, heavily afloat,
I run the river rapids
we know only by effect:
smoke chugging downwind,
apple boughs swinging
their fruit like censers,
the heat mirage gusty
over Lake Cayuga
when, as now, it's flat steel
burning in the sun.

Below me, planes sit nose up
on the airfield, like energy resting.
Only cloud-puffs
high above. At 3,000 feet,
hard a-tilt, I stall,
and a warning buzzer screams
like a marmoset loose
in the cabin, the hull trembles,
shudders twice, like a woman
gently coming, then nestles
straight down toward quilted green
and bedrock, till I get wind
of the right attitude

for lying long on the air,
and land like someone tripping
over toys in the darkness:
stagger, lurch, recovered fall.

But late at night,
still awake in the birdless,
starless black of my bedroom,
I am the moon
rinsed with glitter,
floating full over a poky
and obedient land,
I am motion unmasked
by a wafer of steel,
I am lift made visible,
I am a dancer
with starched coattails for wings,
I am the mouth of a river
whose source is the sky,
I am trembling and hot
from this power-on stall,
I am flight-luscious,
I am kneeling on air.

SPACE SHUTTLE

By all-star orchestra, they dine in space
in a long steel muscle so fast it floats,
in a light waltz they lie still as amber
watching Earth stir in her sleep beneath them.

They have brought along a plague
of small winged creatures, whose brains are tiny
as computer chips. Flight is the puzzle,
the shortest point between two times.

In zero gravity, their hearts will be light,
not three pounds of blood, dream and gristle.
When they were young, the sky was a tree
whose cool branches they climbed,
sweaty in August, and now they are the sky
children imagine as invisible limbs.

On the console, a light summons them
to the moment, and they must choose
between the open-mouthed delirium in their cells,
the awe ballooning beyond the jetstream,
or husband all that is safe and tried.

They are good providers. Their eyes do not wander.
Their fingers do not pause at the prick
of a switch. Their mouths open for sounds
no words rush into. Answer the question
put at half-garble. Say again
how the cramped world turns, say again.

LINDBERGH

For Martin

Half his life he parachuted
from open cockpits in swamp fog,
and the other madly scouted
for where forced landings might work.
It was a tic, his mind painting crashes
as he flew (knowing pilots lived
only an average 900 hours aloft),
while at the same time eagle-eyeing
the stagnant autumn of the fields,
the village life which, as a farm boy,
he knew from the soil up,
to invisible rivers and culverts of air.

Lost, he'd buzz a country to see
what language the store signs spoke,
then reclimb the stairs of flight
to where he loved being a hermit
in a wooden cabin in the clouds.
He always carried a Minnesota boyhood
with him: that frozen winter quiet
so raw he felt a trespasser: the ocean
glaring white and inhuman far below
with enormous cakes of jammed ice,
as he steered alone by a compass
reflected in a lady's compact mirror.

He figured plane and heart would never quit
("How can a whirlwind stall?"),
never feared the wind streaming
at tornado speed over fuselage and wing,
nor the silk he would blossom
to the ground in so often,

as if rehearsing a final cocoon.
Above all, there was no mystery
to life's steepest thrill:
the stick vibrant in his hand,
a quart of stagger in the engine,
death stowed away in every bolt and copper wire,
all existence reaching from one horizon
to the next: spangled, perilous,
interflowing, dumb: in the same instant
supreme and completely without value,
hung on nothing, a few valves and a strut.

FREEING THE EVERGREENS

Weeks after an ice storm glazed
the poplar limbs and bearded everything,

even piled ghostly birds' nests with chickadees
of snow, as if they'd been carved

for a champagne banquet, and jacketed
lean trees with ice (sunlicked,

they seemed to have streaming colds),
we sadly watched our cushion-yews

and evergreens hunch lower and lower
under freeform ice, heard tiny branches

crack like wishbones, saw the delicate
green feathers knuckle under,

pine needles jell, like fossils into rock,
until neither of us could bear

the vicarious agony; panic ruled
and, setting out with brooms and shovels,

we thwacked the branches clean,
filled the yard with slagheaps of snow

as we dug out the bittersweet
and the matted ivies, lifting vines

snakewise over a broom handle
to fluff their ice-bedraggled creepers,

untied the weeping aspen's arms
and, out front, freed the evergreens

crouching under an impossible burden,
stoop-shouldered as pyramid builders

and nearly crippled for all their beauty,
one by one walloped icebergs to smithereens,

uncovering branchfork and tender shoots,
until at last the crushed limbs let fly,

danced in the air, flexed, stretched,
and we could amble indoors for a cup

of something hot, feeling as relieved
as the trees, and as silent:

not needing to voice an instinct
so blatant, so terror-packed, so close to home.

IN THE SILKS

The alarm sounds. The starting gates are empty,
there are no crowds, the track is clotted mud,
there is no finish line, there are no jockeys,
and, anyway, the horses are unrideable.

Nonetheless, at the bell all her muscles tense,
she leans to the jagged withers in her chair,
and her hand grips something wandlike and hard,
a man's body, or a memory, either one a whip.

A RED CARILLON WHOSE BERRIES
ARE BELLS

Because rain fell early
and long this summer, the yard
spawned hundreds of wild strawberries:
pendent hearts
below a canopy of leaves,
whose sawtooth edge we learned
to spot from afar,
but had to search for in sweat weather
when a porridge-white sun
made them fruit low
in the cool hutch of the grass.

Some grew no larger than a wart,
or a kernel; others, fingernail-size,
we called "huge,"
weighing them on an open palm
like garnets
fresh from the lapidaries' quarter
in Tangier. Overripe,
some looked too bruised to touch,
but here and there
one grew perfect to form:
crusted with small seeds,
roly-poly, and symmetrical,
the textbook strawberry, *Fragaria*
(fragrant, sense-swilling),
ready for the margins
of a dictionary, and our plates.

Each day, before dinner,
we preened the lawn, crouching,
and swishing a gentle hand
over miniature orchards:

succulent, fat fruits
    dragging on their stems
        like bright red gizzards.
Those with teeth marks we left,
    sensing disease,
        and knowing how squirrels,
  flushed up with nature's bounty,
    bite once from a berry
and move to the next.
        We dratted their waste,
    but loved their insouciance.

    Few hours soothed us more
all summer than those
    passed in the womb of the day,
        grazing like protohumans
while squirrels foraged alongside,
    using us scarecrows
to ward off the cranky assaults
    of nesting wrens,
  and the rabbits were so tame
we could walk up
    and kick them in the rump.

    Indoors, the wild-strawberry jam
  we made with pectin,
    in rainbow-washed jars,
    fed us many breakfasts
on its rare, pungent curds,
    and the treat of merely being
        among the fruits of summer.

SPIDERS

The eight-legged aerialists
of the tented dawn are up and about.
One leaves a pale orchid,
its exoskeleton, on a twig,
while another fly-casts
against the wind, angling for the leaf
where it would sooner be;
the silk hardens, and it crosses,
tiptoe, the tiny span,
eager to turn mummies
from wing crisp to liquid caramel.

They dote on the tang of quarry,
however they nab it,
with trap door, or purse web,
or keen, jagged fangs,
holding out for that bronchial
shudder of the net, when something
angel-faint, ensnared and hairy
begins the tussle in rigged silk
that can start a greedy eye,
make gossamer hum and, at long last,
even their slack jams quiver.

Last Friday, Dava Sobel, a science reporter
from *The New York Times*, entered the
human chronophysiology laboratory of
Montefiore Hospital to begin 25 days as a
research subject. She is cut off from the
outside world. Freed of the constraints of
the 24-hour day, her body is expected to
establish its own biological day.

—*The New York Times*, June 17, 1980

Dearest friend, dead to me
by time's present fiction:
   I read your plight weekly
      through the dream whorl of print,
how they pox your face and arms
with high-strung electrodes, chart your blood-tides,
     stint you sunlight and chocolate.
A pheasant under glass,
        you are all alone
        yet never alone enough,
     glad-eyed by a legion of mute observers
drawn to the oasis of your vital signs.
    Even your spine begins lower now,
       with a rectal probe:
   in throwback irony, almost a tail.
Eeriest of all, you *feel*
     blood samples leeched from your veins,
       at random moments a quiet tugging.
How can I picture you,
   glass-frail in a glass burrow,
      neon blazing, and all your life signs open,
with only a syringe's steel kiss
     on your birthday, yesterday,

though you told no one. Outside,
            in the fidget and bloom you crave,
        summer is like a new philosophy
    in the air, crammed with wild strawberries
and speckle-throated lilies,
                baby garter snakes
                    lying like pencil leads in the grass,
        and the pool a single blue shudder
            where mallards
            bill-dip and ceremonially mate.
        Sleeping Beauty,
    I read your *Times* article this morning
        and cried; one day,
through no fault of our friendship,
        we'll find ourselves
            a sleep apart forever,
betrayed by the green anthem we love
    and have plighted our word-troth to
        in such different ways,
exiled to the nightmare
        we ferry in our cells,
                rubbed to silence
                    by the thickening waves.

SILHOUETTE

Nightwing, you live in coffins
by day, a mortuary scribe
writing ads for guilt
abstract as leached bone,
with words like "perpetual,"
"always," and "everlasting,"
words too mineral
to use whole with a lover.
To feed your art,
you sell bereavement and brass.
But by night you fly.
Blood draws you out.
Your luxuriant fur glistens
in moonlight, as you steal women's souls.
Earthbound, they come
to sup with you in mid-air,
to give up reflection,
to learn to travel light,
as you roam the quiet spirals
of the world, squashing blossoms
against their pale necks.

Tonight, the air's a cool, slick whisper
to be flown, a benediction
of damp. Everything is at stake.
But all my pelts are twitching tight.
Already moths are beating
in my veins. Love, come drive
your purple fangs in steep,
and jolt me from my flesh tonight,
let me earn my wings.

ICE DRAGONS

In a museum we find them
where they fell:
ichthyosaurus
with seven dragon whelps
in her belly;
sail-backed stegosaurus,
an armor-plated goon
wielding ratchety paws
and eye-coddling breath.

A pinafore of scales,
the sauropod toddles,
fanning its tail
through the mud
as it vamps
from bayou to sandpile,
teeth big as loaves,
a rosebud for a brain.

Another dips
a gravy-boat head to drink,
while bird-monsters
on shoe-leather wings
snuff the quickness
from a shrew.
Squat lizards spit bile,
and baggy-throated tots
trot after prey
with pipette-like claws.

Did they live on to test
Galahad and St. George?
Did they feel
the sudden whammy

of a global gasp?
We blizzard guesses
at their habitat.
We puzzle who
or what's to blame.
Only the bare bones
of a life remain.

IN A SCIENCE-ILLUSTRATOR'S APARTMENT

For Sally Landry

Laundry the sign dins
by her front window,
as though the downstairs proprietor
eyed her at work
laundering a newt's bright web
with black stipples
to draw a fluxy view
of *Diemictylus viridescens.*
$500. For a Boston editor.

Upstairs: black washers,
rubbery as the eggs of a salamander,
sit unused in a box
while the faucet drips.
Mike sleeps; his drafting table
heaves with clutter—
books to design, new jazz albums, a cap. . . .

In the kitchen,
bananas hang bruiseless
on a string, sweetening
at the window sill.
Frameshop bills cling
to the refrigerator door
by an old swimming schedule
and a calendar cued
to outside events.
Her mother's recipe
for homemade prune bread
scents the counter
with the loaf it guarantees.

Leafy plants convalesce
in a south window.
Fishes, fin-perfect
in modeling clay, double
as ad hoc paperweights.
Pillageable books on everything.
Tea leaves, bay leaves.
Color charts of herbs,
sand dunes and wild flowers.
A stretch of purple columbine
drying in a noose.

Underfoot: sounds of argument
jar late into the night—
slamming, squalling, rhythmic dares.
An antique dealer
squeaks old wood
across the sidewalk,
puts out a bookcase,
like a tomcat, for the night,
curbs an unsellable chest
and three chairs:
alms for the thieves.
Bus stop and church chime
on the quarter hour.

Atoms of ink, points of dark,
her dots rim the fallow
pastures in a shape
to draw earwig, lousewort,
bottled gentian, porpoise,
australopithecine man,
then swap figure for ground:
not frog chassis now
but all the space frog-atoms
don't ignite, as if the frogs

penned on her foyer wall
were there just to hail
the universe of things not-frog.

Sally runs a barrette
through her loose auburn hair,
fixes a blue, all-day
flame under the coffee
dripping through a filter
delicate as flesh,
watches a drop fall
into the quickening swill
black as the magic
of a million stipples,
preens her pen shaft
with thin, deft fingers,
then chooses
the day's perfect nib.

TO VILLA-LOBOS IN WINTER

Night falls: a panther
springing.
On a black branch
swarmed over by stars,
an albino moon
rigs its parrot wings
then glides away
while icicle vines
drip in the sweat and tremble of the night.

Reptilian waterfalls
twist and freeze,
drooling ice down each rock face.
It would remind an Aztec
of his white-bearded gods
Bochica or the ousted Quetzalcoatl
who, vowing he'd return, did as Cortés,
a blue-eyed apparition on horseback,
wild for booty and Christ,
this time drawn from a far darkness
to these pagan depths
ropy with gold,
croaking with demons,
hot with gem flowers
set in green bezels
and blood swilled from vein to sky.

Tonight creeps
like the black diamonds on a snake.
Out of gorges, tortured winds
shudder and moan,
then fill with the hideous
panting of the gods.
Silver amaryllis,

the streetlamps bud high.
Mud gore cakes the road.
Under the parrot moon,
soughing a pink eye as it planes
over farm and settlement,
like a knife-edged idol
so chaste, so delicate,
there will be no waking from
this oblique dream of night.

Z O Ë

Ultimate immigrant,
who passed through the Ellis Island
of your mother's hips,
with a name slit loose
from its dialect of cell and bone:
welcome to the citadel of our lives.
We listened for the hoofbeats
(your heart) for nine months
and then your mother nearly died,
hospitably, to give you light.

Like an Hawaiian princess,
you are carried everywhere,
on a litter, in a carriage,
by the arabesque of one's arm.
Your feet have never touched ground.
You, who can't even roll over
when you want, creamy little tyrant,
control the lives of all around you.

Sound leaps from your face
and your ribs quake
each time the downy world chafes.
Last week, you first smiled
because grownups acted silly.
Things elude you, but you can grasp
absurdity already.

By mistake, you suck your wrist
instead of Mother's nipple.
We laugh. With your operatic cries,
and Michelin-man pudge,
and seepages from below,

and eyes alert as twin deer,
you have no sense of self whatever.

Zoë Klein, goddaughter
with a hybrid name,
living in the soft new crook
of your mother's arm,
with a face like a Dalai Lama's
or a small Neanderthal's,
born out of a dream by two,
you live a dream by halves now:
slumbrous, milky-breathed.

In time, love will answer questions
you didn't raise. A belled marvel,
the cat of your inquiry, will stalk
through a world brighter
and more plural than you guess,
where a baby's fingerprints,
loopy weather systems, one for each tip,
will leave you spellbound

that matter could come to this.

PATRICK EWING TAKES A FOUL SHOT

Ewing sweating,
molding the ball
with spidery hands,
packing it, packing it,
into a snowball's
chance of a goal,
rolling his shoulders
through a silent earthquake,
rocking from one foot
to the other, sweating,
bouncing it, oh, sweet
honey, molding it,
packing it tight,
he fires:

floats it up on one palm
as if surfacing
from the clear green Caribbean
with a shell
whose roar wraps around him,
whose surf breaks
deep into his arena
where light and time
and pupils jump
because he jumps

LADY FAUSTUS

I

Devils be ready! My curiosity
   stalks the outpost of its caution,
      and soon I'll swap anything
   from savvy to soul
         for one year's furlough
smackdab in the sleaziest lay-by
      you've got. Take me at my word,
   and now, if you like, before night
digs its purple claws in deep.
      Like spilled pollen,
   sun coats the horizon: raw heat
         fitful as a cautery.
I, too, am burning with a lidless flame.

II

         Bluefall after twilight.
Mud and snow hyena-speckle the road.
      Through a cataract of frost
rimming the window, I browse
         a tiptilted moon, and shake loose
the predatory gaze of two planets.
      Jets crossing like motorboats
between the stars
         seem only a footstep from each
            port of call, a few fathoms perhaps
               to a way station
         tucked under the hem of night—
a viper's den, a Marrakesh
         full of low-life and baubles

mind never dreamed of, rickety hostels,
      banks and beaneries,
   phantoms that clack down the streets
like dice, artists and hucksters,
    grog-shops and depots,
the misguided, the lost, and the shanghaied.

III

    And in that circus mix
where merchants jaw with madmen
   neither men nor mad, I want to dawdle,
 slouched on the curb,
    or strolling ribtight alleys
 that ravel like twine;
 watching jewelers thrill metal
     to carve steel netsukes,
and handymen work miracles
    with stupefied wood;
 learning alien artforms and lingoes;
gaping at creatures
     gaping as spellbound at me,
 pirouette for pirouette,
our eyes fumbling one another
     like pubescent children;
 hearing traders gabble and sign
  an argot spiky as hieroglyphics
   moaned; talking shop
with gauchos from Aldebaran; clapping eyes
  on new and unimagined
    monotonies.

IV

   My heart's no émigré;
the glib traffickings of a squirrel
  can detain me for hours.

So, too, the mud runes left by a newt.
      I try my goodwill on resident aliens
         like the earthworm, or the apple.
    I know so little about an oyster's logic,
or why slugs mate acrobatically
         from slime gallows.
      Earth isn't small enough for me
to exhaust. Why covet mind-teasers
         lightyears away?

     A kennelled dog croons in my chest.
      I itch all over. I rage to know
  what beings like me, stymied by death
and leached by wonder, hug those campfires
        night allows,
      aching to know the fate of us all,
wallflowers in a waltz of stars.

LANGUAGE LAB

Doing Spanish, a young girl
resumes her lament, briskly,
in a blood-chilling monotone,
"My father is very sick,
he is growing thin and pale.
Yes, my mother is sick, too,
and we are terribly worried . . ."

For half an hour, a slim
marzipany voice renders color,
fruit and weather in French.
He orders lunch in a café,
then his mood sours. "I was hungry!"
he moans to his tape recorder
and, mispronouncing only one vowel,

says instead: "I had a woman!"
Sniggers from the Belgians
and Ghanaians. A black face
drifts round the booth wall
like a nimbus. "*Faim,* not *femme!*"
He wags a long finger.
"Bad trouble you mix them."

Hunched over a machine,
a Syrian mutters, "I am *not*
your sister. I am nobody's sister . . ."
A Bolivian boy waves
from a corner seat, his teeth
fiery in the bomb-bright neon.
"Hola, Diana!

How's your sick family today?"
His new English wobbles

like a first bicycle.
" 'Bout the same," I answer,
dragging off my headset,
"Mom's dying; dad's still
in that same auto wreck."

"I'm sorry, so terribly sorry,"
a Korean vows, as if telling
Hail Marys, "so sorry,
so terribly sorry, so sorry . . ."
while a spiky redhead repents
in Portuguese for all the heresy and lust
she looks forward to.

Only false gods rule
in this Babel of curt pleas
and one-syllable verbs,
where the heart's always blunt
enough to slap a noun on,
and, too willingly, the felt
dissolves in the sayable.

The room swells with an extra
Afghan, Thai or Swede.
And the occasional onlooker,
trying to make sense of it,
finds the world shrunk
to twenty-five bright islands,
an archipelago of madness and regret.

IN A PHILOSOPHER'S COTTAGE

For Alfonso Lingis

Below a quiver of Masai arrows
and a long, flexed bow whose resin
is drying out in central heat,
drying as the oiled limbs of its owner
never will in the sultry memories
a few photographs renew,

a lamp made only of an ostrich's left foot
and a single lightbulb
ghosts against an aquarium wall
where striped moray eels—bandannas with teeth—
and a lionfish aflow with poison quills
swoop among blue coral mesas,
between shells brought from reefs
he's dived: the Great Barrier, Sri Lanka,
Yucatán, the Red Sea,
waiting for the live goldfish he feeds them
twice daily from a tank beside his bed,
or with chunks of frozen cod
his two white lavish cockatoos
fight over, perched on his shoulder,
while he guides us round the four corners
of his house, caressing neck feathers
and tufted yellow underwings,
taking care they catch no reflection
from the bathroom, mirrored like a discotheque,
with porcelain-painted chrome,
a stuffed hammerhead shark twirling
at eye level over the bathtub,
and two photos of Nehru drinking water by the door.

His collection of pinned Africans
under glass, butterfly and beetle,

he keeps in a room cool as a light thaw,
a tiny room where the deep-hued calligraphy
of antenna and wing incantates
among the plain, still angles.

There are lingam stones with fossil spirals
sealed within, a Zulu spear by the kitchen door,
where any Zulu would leave it,
mandalas in macabre detail and tints
only nature dyes so intensely
(and that only on frogs),
phallic carvings in ebony to resemble a pistol,
horned penis ornaments from Bali,
African batiks, a war mask from New Guinea
whose knee-length gray hair
charges the stairwell with static electricity,
knife-shaped books carved in Arabic
on palm leaves afray in the dry heat,
and given by young men from Kashmir or Calcutta,
a sacred jeweled Tibetan knife,
its blade forged from meteorite
(he winces when I touch it, sets it gently down),
fossilized rhinoceros teeth on rawhide,
a snakeskin vest from the ten snakes
whose livers he took with rice wine
in Tibet as a cure for impotence,
a typewriter beside a half-written essay
on causality, mother-of-pearl dinner plates,
anisette and cognac, a dozen photo albums he never shows.

Winter is a country he hasn't toured
for ten years. When he comes home, his life
is too eccentric to grasp: the months
spent picking vermin in a Thailand jail,
or deep in the exotic-erotica of Bali.

"How was your summer?" a colleague asks
who hasn't seen him for fifteen years.

Al has large, expensive picture books
of body ornament and regalia:
Leni Riefenstahl walking hand in hand
with a seven-foot Bantu, she in make-up,
bleached hair, and western clothes,
he in penis-thong and ochers;
they are strolling like any couple
on a hot Parisian evening, in paints and pomades.

Living among his artifacts,
he is living within his insides, turned inside out,
his house a form of body ornament
he applies inch by inch, its shaman rule
as unknown to bangled East as to suntanned West.

He pricks open his house,
fills a bole with ash, and then another,
until the raised marks connect into scars
dark as nightfall on the Kalahari,
scars winged, permanent and stiff, but chosen.

RIVER LIGHT

When boat lights flick on at dusk
the eye nimbly orders them
into constellations: a sky menagerie
as the fog roams in.
Arabs would have picked out
the ocher and the blue stars
naming them Fomalhaut, Rigel or Vega,
so nomads could spell their exile
with grains of light, and sense
even in the far-flung mazes of sand
other lids closing to the same lullaby.

Downstream, its steel paws
coated in river oil, a bridge arches
a sooty back against the night,
frozen in that delicate stretch forever.
Trinket small, a hefty machine
stands below, where it was left at 5:00 P.M.,
its limbs jutting out
like the crab of some metaphor
ready to pince life and drag it into view.

The men who work its arms
in the short hours after dawn
when blue does a veil dance
over the water, and sunlight throbs
each rivet into place,
in their private moments
away from the whistle-hoot and holler
do they love the architect of that bridge,
or what he loved?

LINES WRITTEN IN A
PITTSBURGH SKYSCRAPER

It has taken me three years
to come to this view.
I know now that the body
is a river, whose bones and muscles
and organs are flowing.
I have watched their shapes
in the molded Allegheny,
contained and onrushing, below bridge
after bridge vertebra to the Ohio,
a brown river that still
powers the mind, lying long
in the trestle arms of this city
whose sentence is hard labor.

Eye level atop a church
across the street, St. Benedict the Moor
stands open armed and giant,
his back turned to the fuming
of a ghetto where some evenings
the brightest vision
is the flash of a streetlamp
on a jogger's white Nikes.

At night, the red sirens
spinning mute across the river
converge like pulsars
at some accident or crime.
An hour later, one pulls off,
hovers at a distance.
All is gesture and sign.

My students are the children
of coal miners, who watch the ground

swallow their fathers each day,
sometimes even digesting
the trapped men, turning their bones
back into lime, into coal.
It is the oldest fear:
that Earth may recall you.

Along the top of Mount Washington
lies a stole of color
unnatural to sky. Twilight's blue collar.
But the mountains are a fishing
village: steep, hearty, and solid.
At night, the lights and stars
from my window make the cityscape
an Ethiopian bride. As cars bolt
around a curve of streetlamps,
their shadows flash from under them
like sprung souls. And the river
churning its wet whispery thighs,
the river pouring blood dark
under the bridges, in the river
I find my astonished limbs
and all the stateless gels within me,
carnal, mute, wholly flowing,
unburdened toward a distant shore.

THE RUMORED CONVERSATION WITH
ONESELF CONTINUES IN PITTSBURGH

and also a city with quiet pockets
stashed in the hubbub, like this one,

riverside at the base of the cablecars,
where we speak softly about time and space,

two rivers rushing from us as the Ohio does,
whose source is the Point we watch

from Frank's old Chevy, as warm Monongahela
and mountain-iced Allegheny merge blueblack

to vanish braided at the horizon.
What with ground glow, and flecks of city shimmer,

these water streets have more spangle
tonight than the sky. No meteors either,

though the Lyrids are past due.
The moon is nowhere; a hunch in the blackness.

Frank demonstrates its path on steering wheel
and jutting stick shift, telling the lunar opus

so deftly simple, I want to cry.
It's the way Pittsburghers play basketball,

or study Rilke: forging the rudest given
into calm, daily wages, mixing mill and bar

with the *Origin of Species,* discussing Proust
in the stands before a hockey match,

knowing the mind is a hard, slick muscle
toned by thought. And when I confess

that I've been thinking about cuffs all day,
how our joints are cuffs a-swill with fluid,

and how the shape of cuff and bone-end
rule what sort, and how much, motion

will happen, and how the muscles
are bundles of string, across and through

and about the joints, at a twitch
hitching up the marionette of our bones,

for once I feel stark raving sane,
as we sit beneath the small lean-to of wonder,

letting our minds flicker quietly together.
We are talking about drift, our own

and the continents' that clashed like stallions
to be Colorado or Tibet; how women

are marsupials; and early man thought fire
an animal he could only capture.

This is not an odd way to pass evening
in the largest inland riverport town,

but how strange to chat blithely about space
travel, in a Chevrolet whose back seat

sounds like a broken dinette set,
and mauled front seat looks driven to hysteria.

Across the river, a sandstorm of light:
buildings, arc lamps, staggering cars—

too dazzling for any one eyeful to snare.
Somewhere in the lit Oz of a city hospital,

a surgeon is breaking open the shrouded box
of a woman's chest, and reaching

a gloved hand into its snug, lonely muscle,
while she dreams of standing with Julius Caesar

across from the delta skyscrapers
and barges, the train unzipping the night

at such speed, the tunnels and waterworks,
the time-and-motion boys, the computers,

and steam rising from the street vents,
rising from the single sweat gland

under the city, above which a million people
sleep through all the tiny lay-offs

in the cell, dream in the silent architecture
of nerve and bone, people who have not yet forgotten

how to wish, who are awed by the space shuttle,
but not by their own throbbing honeycomb of light

bridging three rivers and gyrating to eye's limit.
She would stand him, mouth agape,

under the moonless sky, across from night-burning mills
spewing raw fire back at the blackness,

across from a city whose incandescence
obscures even the most frantic stars.

Near the goal, head sunk into his shoulders
    as he sprints, Chinaglia takes the ball
        spat at his feet,

dribbles it around a thatch of yellow shirts
    and, sliding between the legs
        of two defenders, belts it hard

into that caged, invisible *something*
    beyond the green reason of the field,
        in the netted calm no one enters.

The home crowd's ear-splitting rant
    grows seismic. Screams blur
        to wind howl and cymbals.

A jig-step. Chinaglia raises his fists
    as laurels. In a waking faint,
        he gallops round the pitch,

leaping, as if lovesick,
    into Marinho's arms, leaping
        to the hypnotic boom of the crowd.

GOLDEN SECTION, GIANTS STADIUM

I

The mind wakes to a whistle
blown in the flesh, whose pea the mind is,
wakes and flows down being's slipway,
then *knows* the sheers of river light,
bridge-rivets and factories,
and raw, panting jungles so humid
the snakes hang straight down, ghettos,
and parkways where dogs salute trees
and picnickers laze on gingham squares
under the lightly buzzing stars.

O the mind, the spidery mind
on whose web the flies of meaning walk.
Nature neither gives nor expects mercy,
but the mind quests to be fit, to be seemly,
and fears second (dying is first)
to become just as plural as all it surveys.
So the autos of habit pull up
to each club at the prescribed hour.
So tidy moments of rapture unfold in the dark.
So the moon rises like a fat white god.

II

Who can know the dervish rhythms
of the mind that whirls for truth
in odd ports-of-call: a New Jersey stadium
whose dry surplus is autumn, late at night,
when the Morse code of the galaxy
pales behind the fainter lights,
and, gifted with the breezy rhetoric
of his legs, a tall, willowy Beckenbauer

swivels, bluffs, and floats long passes,
running upfield among spoon-hipped Latins
playing soccer as if their sun could never cool.

Those tense men in mild weather
who hive and swarm, flying dense circles
around the ball's white flower
to ply the queen of wins with the honey
of their fatigue—for them, defeat lies
in the open scream of a goal-mouth,
and cheers rush like surf breaking
on the bony shoulders of their private sea.

Speak to me, Beckenbauer, about the rhythm
of the mind that searches for perfect order
in imperfect places: art galleries and polling booths,
books, sin-bins, and churches:
and can turn even ceremonial violence
to the mercy of a workable peace.

Reverse Thunder

(1988)

SISTER JUANA INÉS DE LA CRUZ, HEARING THAT HER LOVER, GIORGIO, HAS DROWNED

Mexico, 1694

No, not dead, say "lost," but not dead,
say caged with creeping and spitting
jungle horrors that coat the night
like colored vapors on a glass,
but not dead. Dead, so gong-rich
and familiar, the last stroke at midnight
severing every yesterday from today.
The word is the cot of a corpse: dead.
Giorgio, in the bulging cipher
of his grave. Oh, coarse, unsubtle world
to squander such a fortune in the green
bowels of your sea. How shall I walk
from here to there without him,
when the staff of his love led me on,
steadied me. Never again to sit with him
under a night poxed with stars,
never again to find his hand, scuttling
across the blanket like a wayward crab,
never again to gallop through sedgy fields
by his side, a thick vapor of wild scallions
in the air, his laugh realer than the horizon.
"Dead," you said, and not some other word,
some clot of sounds that means reprieve?
Or perhaps I dreamt him and all of it.
Once in the courtyard, there, I traced
the shadow of a bird across the grass,
knowing by its shadow it was a bird.
If asked what flew, I would have answered "bird";
but suppose it was a kite, or bit of linen,
suppose it was a leaf, or something else unknown,

a mirage, a stilted wish upon a wing.
There was a man named Giorgio?
A man with whom, and knowledge, I lay,
letting the white fever fill me,
whose white fever I could not have said,
so much like brothers were they.
I remember, by the ocean at Veracruz,
tilting my head far back as we loved,
how clouds tumbled across the sky
like bags of light. Once, only sleep
exiled me from him; and, in the morning,
I'd wake to see his hand hovering
over me like a bird of prey
choosing the best place to land.
How shall I inquire, when he was so curious?
How be merciful, when he was so kind?
How create, when he was so full of art?
How eat and drink without the tonic
of his charm? No, the busier I am
the more I will think of him.
Look there, that light dancing on the floor
like a trembling beast. Even the light
has life, and Giorgio has none.
Giorgio dead, and in a carnal circus,
prey to all the mauve hucksters of the deep
who are silently conning him
out of his cells, under a wide green wink.
The filthiest snout in a burrow has life,
black scabs rolling bits of dung have life,
a clamshell tied together by a yawn,
mosquitoes stilting disease across a pond,
mean men bellying from their dens to strike,
my God, even witless plants
droning green anthems in the sun
have life! Count and critter have life!
And Giorgio is dead. Say the world has stopped,

time floats like a scum on dead water,
time swirls like a collop of sand.
My world that seemed so rich before him,
once I knew him, was not enough.
It changed from a moss that lived
only on air to an Orient of petals.
On the long peninsula of my life,
in whose swamps and meadows flocked tribes
of gorgeous, low-nesting birds,
suddenly love built an aviary—
gone now, flooded back to the sea.
Motion is all, and he will be inert.
He will be a lull where a life was.
He will be a neverthriving of hopes.
He will be less than an inkling.
His mind that could contemplate itself, even,
won't contemplate the shy hooves
of a goat. What is life,
that it could include this misery,
as well as those radiant flowers outside?
Giorgio is gone, beyond wish,
beyond dredging, and I am alone again
with my solitary mania, but worse,
for knowing it could be otherwise.
Death, that drank the sun from his sky,
you may as well come feast on mine:
scrape off the colored bark of daylight,
and milk the lilies of the night,
for, like Giorgio, I'm lost at sea,
watching, helpless, as the world empties.

THE ARCHBISHOP OF PUEBLA WEIGHS SISTER JUANA INÉS DE LA CRUZ'S PASSION FOR STUDY

Mexico, 1692

I am no Ramses flogging the nuns of Zion
to heap blocks of stone in a wilderness
of faith. I am no rod of the Lord,
from whose cap pour plagues of toad and locust,
but a mild, much-maligned, faithful servant
of the Lord, who must answer for many souls
in this province. She wishes to learn?
Let her learn! I don't object to her learning.
The hearing ear and the seeing eye,
the Lord made both of them, says Matthew.
If only she would do it discreetly
in the convent's shade, away from the hot
wicked humors of the world,
if only she would do it in moderation:
sip some learning to be cordial perhaps,
but not grow drunk, wild, and unruly from it.
A woman should take the pill of knowledge
in half doses, lest it strain her soft nature,
lest it roughen her mild ways
with a too-manly appetite, lest it bud
in her like the gland of a civet
and attract the lower senses that slobber
and quicken, repeling the pure.
I have met this odd bird at prayer
and on the street, and her knowledge
is a growth, a club foot she drags; it stumbles
from under her robes as she walks.
Nor should a mind so amply equipped
for broad faith and the wider sea of salvation
drag to port in every barrio of the world

to career with roustabouts, fools,
and nay-sayers, in the petty hovels
and refuse heaps of a common life.
In a lesser mind, it would be a lesser folly.
They are all trouble, these raucous birds,
who come direct from court and high families,
direct from the spoils and petting
of duped fathers to dance into their vows,
believing they can wheedle salvation from God
as if it were an extra sweet or new ribbon.
Like horseleeches, these daughters
cry only "Give, Give." But the path to salvation
is overgrown, and the jungles snarled high.
They must learn to chop through evil
without wincing, slash at temptation,
scrape away the private poisons
and cleanse the wound with fire,
these women who are born with wounds
in which their own blood rains
like a holocaust every month,
thanks to the disobedience of Eve.
They return to her wickedness,
these unholy sisters,
wrapped all in black,
like rats lurking in their own shadows.
How they sink their teeth
into the apple of the church,
and wish to drive the manly body of the law
to spill itself on the ground for them.
They taint its pure spirit with their fetid blood,
with their filthy, pouring volcanos inside.
That life could hatch in such a mire—
it's disgusting! Like goslings
born out of a swollen, smelly marsh.
You can't put pure wine into a corrupt bottle
and expect it to stay sweet. No, no.

This sister, she needs to be purified,
purified by a worm, a worm of terror
with a long, spiny maw below her gut
working its icy mischief as she sleeps;
she needs to have the cross burned on her tongue
so each word will be cleansed
by the agony of Our Lord; she needs
to be stuffed with lilies dipped in holy oil,
and then the cave of her disgrace sewn shut.
I will make her pure as a benediction,
so she's fit again for men's eyes,
snowy, clean, bloodless, and unstained,
a single white candle burning its wax
on the altar. I will crush the pearl in her hips,
and turn her poppy-red gush
into a single beating faith.
I will blank out the farting trumpet
of her studies, and distill her bubbly spirit
to still wine. I will take an axe
and strike at the root of her,
where false prophets build a tabernacle
and virtue is razed.
Will she squirm? Then I will fasten her
like a nail to a sure place,
so she will not escape, or her flesh will stay.
I will rash her unholy, sin-charred limbs
with a shirt of my own hair
until she begs me to flog her,
questing for pain like a perfect rose.
I will make her soul jump from her body
like a shadow from the sparkling glare
of sunlit water. I will heat her will
like iron in a forge, bend her into a shape
fit for salvation, and quench her slowly,
in stages, the last as she quivers,
deep into the sacred blue vat of Heaven.

AN ITALIAN COURTIER PINES FOR HIS MISTRESS, THE LEARNED NUN, SISTER JUANA INÉS DE LA CRUZ

Mexico, 1692

What a troupe of weeks has come
parading through my life, each more dizzying
and acrobatic than the last. A regatta of days,
full of walks and rides and books
and quiet, illuminated hours during which we spoke
of nearly nothing, nearly everything.
Even her idle chatter has sunlit ways.
If only my wishes were homing pigeons
and I could shed the miles right now. What's a day?
A few hours strapped together by the sun;
she's made mine glide like a pendulum,
dividing and uniting in a stroke,
each moment meeting its double on the run,
till gravity pulls it back again.
But I'm lying. Time doesn't move at all,
it stammers, it gags, it hiccups, it faints,
it throws tantrums, it sleeps till noon.
Time and I are like two ghouls
locked in the coliseum of these walls.
First it whips me with its long moaning hours
in which a minute is a multitude
and nothing can split the armor of a day.
And then I snake its wrist by nimbly picturing her:
the spa of her glance; her wit a whetstone
that sharpens itself; her long fluent fingers.
I think of her dressing in the morning,
when dew is a flat cloud on the grass,
and make the moment last longer
than her dressing does. Clothed in the soft linen

of her books, her old underlinens gone
to ragmen to be pulped for new books,
she is where the books begin and end.
Lucky linen, to have such a muse at hand.

ABOUT THE AUTHOR

DIANE ACKERMAN was born in Waukegan, Illinois. She received her B.A. in English from Pennsylvania State University, and an M.F.A. and Ph.D. from Cornell University. She is the author of three collections of poems, *The Planets: A Cosmic Pastoral* (1976), *Wife Light* (1978), and *Lady Faustus* (1983), and most recently of *Reverse Thunder: A Dramatic Poem* (1988).

Her books of nonfiction include *Twilight of the Tenderfoot* (1980), *On Extended Wings* (1985), and the bestselling *A Natural History of the Senses* (1990). She has received the Academy of American Poets' Peter I. B. Lavan Award, and grants from the National Endowment for the Arts and the Rockefeller Foundation among other prizes and awards. Ms. Ackerman has taught at a variety of universities, including Washington University, New York University, Columbia, and Cornell. She is currently a staff writer at *The New Yorker,* and is working on several books, including *The Moon by Whale Light,* about the world's most fascinating animals. She lives in New York State.